THE COMPLETE GUIDE TO
Western Horsemanship

THE COMPLETE GUIDE TO WESTERN

HORSEMANSHIP

J. P. Forget

Howell Book House
New York

Dedicated with love to my wife Louise
and my son Daniel,
and to my parents,
Albert and Cécile

This book is not intended as a substitute for professional advice and guidance in the field of horseback riding. A person should take part in the activities discussed in this book only under the supervision of a knowlegeable horseman.

Illustrations by Patricia Kemp. All photographs by the author unless otherwise noted.

HOWELL BOOK HOUSE
A Prentice Hall Macmillan Company
15 Columbus Circle
New York, NY 10023

Library of Congress Cataloging-in-Publication Data
Forget, J.P.
    The complete guide to western horsemanship / J.P. Forget.
      p.   cm.
    Includes index.
    ISBN 0-87605-982-5
    1. Western riding.   I. Title.
SF309.3.F67 1995
    798.2'3—dc20   94-39679
                                                CIP

Manufactured in the United States of America
10 9 8 7 6 5 4 3 2 1

Contents

Foreword

It is my pleasure to be writing this foreword for J. P. Forget's book, *The Complete Guide to Western Horsemanship*. J. P. has dedicated his life to teaching equine education, which is how I first met him at Olds College several years ago. J. P. had asked me to come there to do a reining clinic for his students. I found J. P. to be very knowledgeable and to have an intense desire for improvement, both in his students and in himself.

A few years later I went back for a second clinic and then last fall we had an opportunity to ride together for about a week. I was impressed with J. P.'s application of the principles set down in this book. Between the first time I saw J. P. ride and the last time, he had made great improvements in his riding, which indicates to me his understanding of these fundamentals and his ability to apply and teach them.

I have found *The Complete Guide to Western Horsemanship* to be an excellent reference for the beginner, as it is basic and simple to understand, yet at the same time it offers insights the intermediate and advanced rider can appreciate. I sincerely believe that this is one of the most comprehensive books I have seen because it covers basic horsemanship, safety techniques, body positions, hand and leg aids, bits, and finally how to coordinate all of these elements to be effective in the different events in which a rider might want to participate.

The book offers a well-illustrated chapter on the anatomy of the rider's seat, discusses at length the important question of sitting in balance, and lists a number of exercises designed to help riders improve their balance and effectiveness at all gaits. The chapter on the use of seat aids delves into the effective use of this powerful but often misunderstood aid. Bitting aids and the characteristics of the bitted horse are important to the winning rider, and J. P.'s treatment of this subject is most informative.

Another interesting aspect of this book is J. P.'s attention to the rider's psychology. I've not seen this discussed much in horsemanship books, but it is a critical component of the successful horseman. Being an effective horseman takes a certain amount of tenacity and *mental preparation,* and I'm happy to see it discussed. I commend J. P. for putting together such a well-rounded book. I think all riders who are serious about improving their skills will want this book.

The best of luck to you, J. P., as you continue your endeavors in equine education.

Kearny, Nebraska

Doug Milholland
1988, 1991, 1992 NRHA Reserve Futurity Champion
1990 NRHA Futurity Champion

Acknowledgments

Many people played an essential role in the development of this book. It is my pleasure to ackowledge the great contributions of those who supported me and made this book a reality:

My wife Louise and my son Daniel, for their unconditional love through this and other projects. Their sacrifice of themselves, their patience, and their support helped me keep my eyes on the goal and gave me the impetus to see it through.

Greg Lajoie, who, by arranging my first job in the horse industry, opened the door for me to the challenging world of horsemanship and horse training.

Don and Barbara Ellis, for their continuous support, the opportunities they gave me, and for treating me as their son.

Doug Milholland, for supporting this project and writing the foreword.

Sigmund Brouwer, my author friend, for his helpful on-line advice and encouragement—from the budding idea for this book all the way to the end.

Patti Kemp, for her patience and dedication to the drawings.

Ted Gard, for his enthusiastic approach to taking many of the photographs.

Rob Long, my dear friend and English teacher, for his long hours of attentive editing.

Tracy Flynn, for her editing and suggestions.

Sierra Fisher, Pernell Fleck, Jim Freeman, Tiffany Herron, Sara Hooper, Wylda Kristel, Lorna Malnberg, Lisa Mowat, Cherie Petersen, Cindy and Sheldon Soderberg, Elaine Speight, and Julie Verstaen for their roles in the photographs.

Bonnie McAskill, B.A., for her precious help in the section on fitness.

Madelyn Larsen, my editor, for her enthusiasm for the project and her joyful guidance.

And all my students, whose desire to better themselves and their horses became a great motivator for the writing of this book.

Introduction

For years I have coached riders and taught horsemanship and horse training at all levels. And through those years I have felt great satisfaction in seeing riders and students discover the joy of becoming more accomplished riders. The feeling of personal victory that comes from being able to sit the trot correctly is a reward worth seeking. To feel the correct lead on a consistent basis, to sit a sliding stop correctly, to guide a horse around a barrel without losing precious time are all goals riders seek to achieve. And achieving these goals demands a mastery of mind and body that one can apply in other areas of life, whether professional or personal.

Yet ideas must enter the mind before they can be applied. Knowledge gives direction. It outlines the challenges. It places all elements of an activity in focus and perspective. Knowledge makes any activity interesting. Knowledge can lead to uplifting personal victories. Knowledge of horsemanship makes the sport safer to practice and beneficial to your horse's health.

Horsemanship is one of the most demanding disciplines to master. Be prepared for dedicated hard work. Hard work, not in the sense of physically exhausting efforts but rather in the sense of sustained, regular, focused riding of as many different horses as you can fit into your day.

Perhaps you are a rider with other commitments who cannot ride several horses a day for a year to gain feel and experience. Do not give up! You can become an effective, successful, knowledgeable horseperson without quitting your job or neglecting your children.

If mastering horsemanship is your goal, congratulations! This book is designed to help you achieve your goal.

This book gives you the knowledge you need to achieve high levels of competency in horsemanship. It begins with safety rules and takes you all the way to the aids used to ride horses at the advanced level in such sophisticated events as western pleasure, reining, barrel racing, and cutting.

This book not only covers technical aspects of horsemanship—such as how to use your hands, legs, and seat—but also explains how you can use your mind to improve yourself.

Clearly, this book will not make you an expert on horsemanship. Only you and the horses you ride can do that; and they will certainly set high expectations for you. But if you listen to what your horses are telling you and strive to respond to them correctly, you will undoubtedly develop into a very effective horseperson.

PART I

The term *basic,* when used to refer to handling, is somewhat of a misnomer. Although basic handling is fundamental in the sense that it is what should be learned in the first stages of horsemanship, it is essential—something riders should never forget. In fact, poor handling of a horse on the ground creates nervousness and fear. A horse that does not trust human beings while they lead him around the barn or paddocks will not trust them while one sits on his back. This is largely because the people who give him reasons for distrust while handling him are often the same ones who ride him, and their lack of horse sense almost guarantees stiffness and escape under saddle. Therefore, basic handling requires an advanced level of know-how. And this know-how can be acquired only by being around horses and being with other horsepeople who are models of correct behavior and handling.

The lessons in horse sense that you learn from the ground are based on the same principles as those applied on horseback. The patience shown while familiarizing the horse with grooming is the same patience required to give the horse time to develop the strength needed to run a winning barrel race. The rider who has no time to school his or her horse in trailer loading but who instead uses a whip in an abusive way the morning of the show is likely to be the one who jerks the horse's mouth after failing to position him correctly for a lope departure.

So before you read any further, close the book and think of your horse-handling manners. Are you patient, yet expecting a response? Or are you rough and tough, jerking your horse around and giving him little time to respond to your commands? What about your commands? Are they clear to your horse, or do you expect him to read your mind?

Watch other people as they handle horses. You may see in their actions things you need to correct in your own. If you are inexperienced with horses, hang around and watch respected, experienced horsepeople. If you do not understand what they do, ask questions. If you are experienced at handling horses and the horses you handle are quiet and responsive on the ground, they are more likely to perform well under saddle.

The next two chapters outline some principles of horse handling, including those that govern safety, clipping, picking up the horse's feet, and trailer loading. You will find, throughout the book, additional indications of the ways a horse behaves and reacts to the actions of human beings. Also available are several good books on horse behavior, herd instinct, and body language. I suggest that you read them and familiarize yourself with your horse's mind.

CHAPTER 1

Safety

Horseplay is unsafe.

The sport of horseback riding is potentially harmful. It is one of the three most dangerous sports, taking its place alongside automobile racing and motorcycle riding. A horse is a muscular animal that weighs ten times more than a man and is dozens of times stronger. A horse can run up to thirty-five miles per hour. He can slip, stumble, and fall. All of this while the rider's head is as much as eight feet above the ground. Studies show that head injuries are the most frequent and the most severe injuries to befall riders. Concussions are the most common injuries, but many riders have suffered severe trauma with lasting consequences and, sadly, even death.

Prevention is the first step toward safety. The wise rider practices prevention on two fronts: his or her riding dress and tack.

The riding hard hat prevents skull penetration and deformation and reduces energy transfer to the brain in the event of a fall. The hard hat must be well fitted and secure. It should feature an adjustable harness and chin strap. A rider wearing a loose hard hat or one with no chin strap will not benefit from the protection of the head gear. Movement of the hat on the rider's head could aggravate the injuries. Loss of the hard hat before impact offers no protection at all.

Heeled riding boots are of primary importance. No one should ever ride a horse wearing anything less. The heel prevents the foot from sliding through the stirrup and becoming trapped, possibly resulting in a horrible drag. The thick leather of the boot leg offers protection and support from collisions.

Riders must be aware of the hazards of long hair, which can get tangled in branches or in the rider's eyes and impair vision. If your hair is long, braid it or put it up inside the helmet.

A most important step toward safety is taken when a rider begins to understand a horse's mind, how it works and why it reacts as it does. If you are a beginner or an intermediate rider, be sure to ride with an experienced coach. If you are a novice rider, do not ride above your level of ability. If you have difficulty staying on the horse, you are going too fast.

SAFETY ON THE GROUND

Injuries to riders happen not only while riding, but often while preparing for a ride. Keep the following guidelines in mind while working around your horse.

- Always tie a horse short and at eye level to prevent him from stepping over the lead rope.
- Always use a strong lead rope and halter.
- Always tie a horse to a solid object, one he cannot move and that will not break if he pulls back on the halter.
- Never tie your horse close to a strange horse because they may kick at each other.
- Never lead a horse by holding onto the halter.
- Always use a long lead rope when leading a horse. If the horse rears, you can still hold onto the lead shank.
- Use caution in the way you carry the excess lead rope. Do not coil it around your hand; rather, make a figure eight with it.

The quick-release knot is the safest way to tie your horse. Pull the free end of the lead rope through the loop to prevent your horse from untying himself.

Always tie your horse at eye level. Be sure the length of lead rope you set between the halter and the quick-release knot is shorter than your horse's neck.

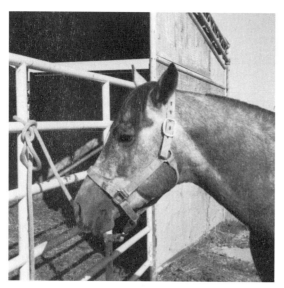

When lungeing or leading a horse, avoid coiling the line or lead rope in your hand. Rather, run it back and forth from the left side to the right side of your hand, forming a loop on each side of it.

- Never lead a horse from behind his shoulder. Rather, always stay between his shoulder and his head.
- When leading a horse into a stall, always go in before him. A horse could squeeze you against the door if you were to walk into the stall beside him.
- Always ask permission before leading a horse through a group of people.
- As you lead a horse, never pull him toward you to turn him. Not being able to see behind himself, the horse could bolt and run over you if something were to scare him. The preferred way to turn a horse is to push him away from you. Then, if the horse were to become frightened, he would run in that direction instead of toward the unsuspecting handler.
- Never wrap the lead rope or reins around your wrist or body. Sadly, people have been dragged to death for breaking this rule.
- Do not try to pull on a lead rope while leading a horse. Doing so will likely cause him to pull back against you. If the horse stops as you lead him, first determine whether he is scared of something ahead. If he is not frightened but needs encouragement to proceed, a quick snap on the lead rope will usually suffice.
- Never walk under a horse's neck or the tie rope. A horse cannot see under his neck and may be frightened when you disappear on one side and reappear on the other. If the horse were to pull back on the halter, he could bounce forward and hit you with his front legs, causing serious injury.
- When moving from one side of the horse to the other while he is tied, stay close to him, keeping one hand on his hip at all times.
- Never approach a horse directly from behind but always at an angle from the shoulder. A horse cannot see behind himself and may kick when startled. If the horse is in a tie-stall and you must approach him from the rear, warn him of your presence by calling him. After he has turned his head and located you with his eye, gently touch him on the croup.

Stay close to his body as you move to his head.
- When picking up a horse's leg, never grab his ankle but rather rub your hand down his leg to make him aware of your intention.
- When turning a horse loose into a large pen or a box stall, always turn him so that he is facing the gate or door. Pull the gate or door closed and then remove the halter. This way, the horse has to pivot before running off, leaving you clear away from him.
- Never turn a horse loose with his halter on. Halters get caught on various solid objects and horses can die trying to free themselves.

Although following these rules does not guarantee that accidents will not happen, doing so will greatly reduce the chances that someone could be injured.

EQUIPMENT

Nothing affects a rider more than an injury suffered while riding horseback. This is particularly true in the case of beginners. Hordes of people have been turned off equestrian sports because safety rules were broken and injuries ensued.

- Keep your head in the clear when bridling a green horse. He may throw his head to avoid the bridle.
- Be sure the saddle pad and cinches are free from dirt and debris. Dirty pads irritate the horse and cause him to act up.
- If you are using a double-rigged saddle, be sure to tighten the front cinch first, then the back cinch. When unsaddling, remember to undo the back cinch first, then the front cinch.
- If your saddle has a back cinch, be sure to have it tight at all times. A loose back cinch can get caught in the brush or a horse could step in it. The connecting strap between the back and front cinches should be in good

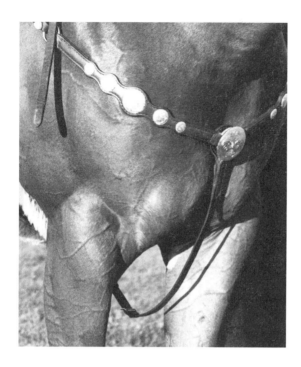

Aside from being completely ineffective, this poor-fitting breast collar is dangerous. A stick or other foreign object could snag the hanging tie-down and cause injury to your horse and to you.

condition and taut when the saddle is cinched down on the horse.

- When saddling, tighten the cinches enough to keep the saddle from turning, then lead the horse a few steps before tightening them enough to mount the horse.
- Never use snap-on reins with running martingales. The ring from the martingale can get hooked on to the snap, irritating the horse and causing him to rear up.
- Replace all Chicago screws with latigo lacing.
- Purchase quality equipment and keep it in a good state of repair. Cinches, latigos, reins,

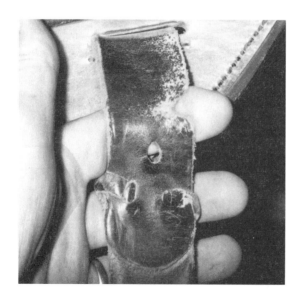

Latigos and cinches should be replaced as soon as they show any sign of wear. This latigo is about to break, potentially causing serious injuries to the rider.

and headstalls usually see the most wear. Check them regularly for (1) loose buckles; (2) worn-out latigo lacing; (3) broken or pulled-through copper rivets; (4) rotten or unravelling cinch; and (5) cracked stirrup leathers.

RIDING

Riders of all levels need to respect a range of rules while on horseback. These rules vary according to the environment riders find themselves in. Be sure to respect the following rules for an enjoyable practice of the equestrian sport.

- If you are a beginner, never ride alone. Always make sure that a more experienced rider is there to coach you.
- Choose a horse whose disposition is suitable for your level of expertise. Spirited, energetic horses are dangerous for a beginner who does not yet have complete control of the commands he or she gives to the horse.
- Never slide your foot all the way into the stirrup when mounting a horse.
- Never mount a horse without first shortening your reins and establishing contact with his mouth. Mounting any horse on loose reins is an invitation to disaster.
- Never mount a horse in a small barn, near a fence, trees, or overhanging structures. If the horse were to move as you mount, you could be injured.
- If a horse obviously has too much energy, it is wise to work him on the lunge line or in the pen before mounting.
- If your horse is frightened by an obstacle, steady him with your hands and legs and give him time to overcome his fear. Do not punish the horse for exhibiting natural fear.
- Ride with your weight on the balls of your feet so that you can easily free your feet from the stirrups if your horse should happen to fall.
- Hold your horse to a walk when riding rough ground, mud, ice, or snow.

- Always walk your horse to and from the stable to prevent him from becoming barn sour.
- If your horse tries to run away, turn him in a circle, tightening the circle until he stops.
- No-smoking rules should be strictly enforced inside horse barns and in areas that contain bedding and hay.

Safety on the Trail

- If you ride alone, tell someone where you are going and when you will be back.
- In wilderness areas, carry a map and compass and learn how to use them.
- Avoid horseplay.
- Avoid riding unfamiliar trails at night.
- Avoid tying your horse to trees. Horses paw the cover off the roots and chew the bark of the trees. Eventually, the trees die and the environment suffers.
- Always keep one horse length between your horse and the one in front. Many horses object to being crowded and will kick.
- If a rider has to dismount for any reason, all other riders should wait until he or she is safely back in the saddle before proceeding. Most horses will not stand quietly to be mounted while the rest of the herd rides off. This could cause problems for the rider trying to mount.
- Do not trot or lope past other horses on the trail. Some horses get excited when others run by them, causing accidents to the less experienced riders in the group.
- If you are riding at the head of a large group, be sure to wait for everyone. Stop when necessary for the last riders to catch up.
- The last rider in the line should make sure that no one gets lost or left behind.
- Do not "ground tie" your horses out on the trail. Most horses do not ground tie and some have not been found for weeks. Leave a halter under the bridle and carry a lead rope.
- Never tie a horse with the bridle reins. They are not solid enough and the bit could cause injury to the horse's mouth were he to pull.
- Lead your horse down steep banks instead of riding him down. Be sure to walk beside him, not in front of him.

- Always use a breast collar and a back cinch when riding in the high country. Your saddle will stay in place better, keeping you from becoming injured and your horse's shoulders and back from becoming sore.
- Do not ride straight up steep hills. Rather, guide your horse back and forth across the face of the hill.
- Remove your tie-down before crossing water. A horse cannot swim when his head is tied down and may fight for his life if he feels the water is too deep.
- Stay away from deep water if you possibly can. Not all horses can swim and some have drowned as a result of being ridden in deep water.
- If your horse starts to swim, get off and stay beside him or behind him, never in front of him: the paddling of his front legs may drag you under water.
- Always cross a fast river by angling your horse down stream.
- In a thunderstorm, always find cover below timberline.

Safety on the Road

- Check with the appropriate agency or department for information regarding riding along the roads in your area. Horse traffic is prohibited on some highways.
- Use the correct hand signals to indicate your travelling intentions: right turn, left turn, and stop.
- Be sure the horse is trustworthy and not afraid of traffic.
- Wear proper attire, including a hard hat. Wrap reflective tape around your sleeves and ankles, and around your horse's tail.
- Avoid riding on roads at night.
- Ride in single file.
- Ride in the same direction as vehicular traffic.
- Obey all traffic signs, lights, and the police.
- Respect private property. Ask for permission to pass through.

TRAILERING SAFETY

Each year many horses, and sometimes their drivers, suffer injuries and even death due to trailering accidents. Many of these accidents can be prevented if the driver performs a simple safety check of his or her rig before departure. Here, briefly outlined, are some of the most important points you should make a habit of checking before you take to the road with a horse trailer.

- Stand to one side of your horse, never behind, when loading and unloading him from a trailer.
- Be sure the area around the trailer offers safe footing. Ice, mud, or otherwise slippery surfaces are dangerous.
- Continually speak to your horse if you have to go into the trailer with him.
- If your trailer is of the two-horse straight-load type, always close the back door before you tie up your horse.
- To unload your horse, always untie him before opening the back door.
- Check your trailer regularly for (1) weak or broken floor boards; (2) broken welds on hitch and door hinges; (3) worn or broken springs, shackles, wheel bearings, and safety chains; (4) low air pressure in tires; (5) worn-out tires; (6) the wiring and connections of lights and brakes; (7) spare tire and tools for changing a tire; (8) broken windows and other sharp objects; and (9) malfunctioning door latches.
- When hauling only one horse, load it on the high side of the road, usually the left side of the trailer.
- Drive defensively, looking ahead to prevent accidents.
- Take all turns slowly. Start and stop very slowly and steadily.
- If the horse you are hauling is halter broke, tie him.

The horse is a living creature with senses and instinct. Few horses will react the same way in a given situation. And riders have different levels of experience, patience, and horse sense. These facts make the safety rules discussed in this chapter even more important.

Clearly, even when all the rules are followed, riders will still fall off horses. However, the number as well as the seriousness of injuries will certainly diminish. Safety is a prerequisite to the enjoyment of any equestrian sport. Let's be mindful of it.

CHAPTER 2

Basic Handling

Correctness in the basics is key to excellence at the higher levels.

Activities such as clipping, picking up feet, and trailer loading are not only important in the development of your horsemanship skills, but essential to the proper management of your horse. In this chapter, I show you how to familiarize your horse with the clippers. I also describe in detail how to bring your horse to load readily and willingly. And I highlight the important points of saddling, bridling, and mounting a horse.

CLIPPING THE FOAL OR ADULT HORSE

Sooner or later, most horses are presented at a show or sale. When that opportunity arrives, the horse's appearance and value are often enhanced by proper grooming. This includes trimming the horse's bridle path, his muzzle, and possibly his ears.

Unfortunately, most riders do not take the time to train their horses to be clipped. Horses usually react violently to the sight and sound of the clippers. Handlers often lose patience and punish the horse. Over time, clipping sessions become more frightening for the horse and even dangerous for the handler.

Horses have good reasons for reacting as they do. Clippers are noisy. They vibrate. They are cold. The horse's instinct is geared toward survival. Naturally, he is scared of the foreign object entering his environment.

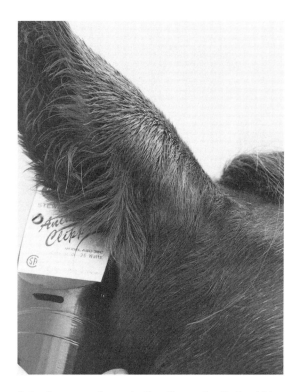

Introduce your horse to the clippers by first rubbing him with them while they are turned off. Your horse will interpret the vibrations as well as the noise and smell of the clippers as danger unless you take the time to show him otherwise.

Training a horse to be clipped is the same, whether he is a foal or a mature horse. The process, called desensitization, requires time and patience. In practical terms, it means that the clipping procedure is introduced to the horse step by step and that the handler makes sure the horse has fully accepted one step before moving to the next.

The first step is to show the horse the clippers without turning them on. Let him smell the clippers. Rub them over his body, neck, poll, ears, and muzzle. When the horse stands quietly as you walk up to him with the clippers, go on to the next step.

Activate the clippers while you stand some distance away from the horse. Move about with them turned on. As the horse relaxes, move closer to him with the clippers turned on.

Acquaint the horse with the vibrations of the clippers by placing your hand between the clippers and his skin. The warmth of your hand and the reduced vibrations will do much to gain the fearful horse's confidence. Do not begin to clip the horse until he has fully accepted the vibrations over his poll, ears, forehead, and muzzle.

You can also condition your horse to the clippers. This is best accomplished by turning on a pair of clippers for five or ten minutes while the horse eats. Eventually, the horse will associate the pleasurable feeling he gets from eating with the clippers. You will save some time this way but should still go through the desensitization process to leave a lasting feeling of acceptance in the horse's mind.

Check the blades before clipping the horse. Dull, misfitting blades pull the hair and irritate the horse.

How much clipping you should do depends on the purpose of the clipping, the conditions in which the horse is stabled, as well as the breed's characteristics. If the horse is to be taken to a show, the bridle path, muzzle, and ears must be clipped. If, on the other hand, the horse is kept outside, clipping the ears, the coronet band, and the fetlocks is not advised because the hair in these places is necessary for protection against the elements and insects.

Each breed has customary requirements as to the length of the bridle path. For Arabians and gaited horses, the trim should be fairly long. For the stock horse breeds, the bridle path usually is trimmed the same length as the horse's ear as it lays on his neck.

Take the time necessary to train your horse to be clipped. Be patient, gain his trust. It is a test of your horsemanship. The horse gives you the marks. Whether you pass or fail will have long-term consequences for him.

PICKING UP FEET

A horse's usefulness is determined by his soundness. Because most soundness problems occur in the lower leg area, it is important that the horse be willing to let a handler pick up his feet. A horse who won't let a person pick up his feet and care for them—including trimming and shoeing—is a dangerous animal with limited use.

Following is a safe and effective method of picking up your horse's feet.

A horse may not let a handler pick up his feet—the most important tool he has for defending himself—for three basic reasons. First, a horse's feet are his protection. With his feet, the horse can run away from danger. He can kick. He can strike. Without his feet to ensure his flight, a horse is at the total mercy of his immediate environment. If that environment is unfamiliar and seemingly unfriendly, the horse will want to keep his feet to himself in case his safety becomes threatened. This behavior is greatly reinforced when a horse has a bad experience while having his feet picked up.

To pick up a hind foot, follow the same procedure as for the front foot. Be sure to stay ahead of the horse's flank if you are not sure how he will react.

To pick up your horse's feet, be sure he is standing relatively square and balanced on all four feet. If your horse has a hind limb deep under his body, it will be difficult for him to stand on three legs and he probably will not let you hold his foot for very long. To pick up his front foot, follow these steps: (1) Face the rear of the horse. (2) Place the hand closest to the horse on his shoulder. Were the horse to become startled and move toward you while you were bending down, the hand on the shoulder and perhaps some stiffness in the arm would cause you to be pushed away by the horse. (3) Run your other hand down his leg, all the way to the fetlock. (4) Press gently on your horse's shoulder, asking him to shift his weight to his other limb as you flex this one.

Avoid taking the horse's hind limb back as soon as you get it off the ground. Your horse will be more accepting of the procedure if you first bring his foot under his torso, then set about taking it behind him for cleaning.

Another reason horses will refuse to have their feet picked up is that a horse's feet are in a blind area. Often, because of the way he stands or because of his conformation, the horse cannot see the handler's actions down around his legs. Unfortunately, many horse owners do not know this and often punish the horse for moving around when he is only trying to position himself to see what the handler is doing.

A third reason a horse will be afraid of having a foot picked up is a matter of equilibrium. It is not natural for a horse to stand on three legs. A horse stands on three legs when he walks and when he lopes. He stands on two legs as he trots. But a horse never stands motionless with a foot off the ground unless something or someone holds it up.

It is never too late to train your horse to have his feet picked up. It is much easier, however, if you do it as you halter train your weanlings. Training a horse to have his feet picked up should be an integral part of the gentling process necessary for all foals. The method is the same whether you are dealing with a newborn foal or an adult horse.

Following is the proper procedure for picking up a horse's front foot:

1. Stand by his front leg, facing the rear of the horse.
2. Place the hand closest to the horse on his shoulder.
3. Run the other hand down his front leg. This is very important for your safety. Never reach down and grab a horse's lower leg without first rubbing your hand down his leg to give him notice of your intention. If the horse you are working is not accustomed to having his feet picked up, this may be as far as you can go. Do not try to pick up this horse's foot until he lets you rub your hand all the way down his leg. If the horse moves some, let him. If he bends his neck to have a better look at what you are doing, let him.

4. Once the horse is comfortable with you at his side and rubbing his leg, apply pressure to his shoulder to transfer his weight to the far side, then pick up his foot. Be careful not to pull the horse's foot out to the side. This would surely scare a green horse or a foal.
5. If picking up the foot of a green horse or a foal that is not familiar with the procedure, hold the foot up for a few seconds and then place it down. To place the foot down, reverse the procedure in Step 4. It is important that you place the foot down rather than drop it. Dropping the foot sends a painful jolt up the horse's leg and can cause lameness.

To pick up a hind leg, proceed as follows:

1. Facing the rear of the horse, stand by his ribs. Never get past the horse's flanks. If he were to kick, he could hurt you much more than if you position yourself closer to the rib cage.
2. Place the hand closest to the horse on his hip.
3. Run the other hand down the back of the horse's hind leg.
4. Cup the fetlock in the palm of your hand, keeping your thumb and fingers together.
5. Pull the foot forward under the horse's belly. If you are working with a green horse or a foal, hold the foot in that position for a few seconds and then place it back on the ground.
6. When the horse is relaxed and balancing himself well on three legs, step under the hind leg and move to the rear until the cannon is perpendicular to the ground. Do not pull the leg off to the side. This would put the horse off balance and scare him.

Hold the hind leg across your thighs to clean the foot.

Many horses refuse to have their hind feet picked up because the handler omits the very important step of bringing the foot under the horse's belly before stretching it to the rear. Therefore, the horse does not have the opportunity to balance himself and tries to free his hind leg. The handler often loses patience and punishes the horse. The horse gets scared and becomes dangerous.

Many people use a hoof pick or rasp to get a horse to pick up his foot. They poke his heels or fetlock until he picks up his foot. This is not a recommended practice because it causes the horse to become nervous when someone touches his lower legs.

Gain your horse's confidence as you work with his lower legs. Let him know you are going to pick up his foot. Give him a chance to balance himself as you hold the foot up. Your horse's health will benefit, as will yours and that of your farrier.

TRAILER LOADING

We watched from a distance as the young teenager tried to load his chesnut gelding. He began by trying to lead the horse into the trailer. The gelding came within two meters of the trailer, then stopped.

The boy pulled on the halter shank. The horse pulled back, dragging the lad out of the trailer. The boy tried again. Again the horse dragged him out of the trailer. The third time, the gelding pulled back so violently that the boy dropped the lead rope.

Someone caught the horse and handed him over to the boy's mother.

She got a bucket of oats and attempted to load the horse by spilling the oats on the floor of the trailer. The horse ate the oats as far as he could reach without stepping into the trailer, then turned his head away and refused to move.

We went for dinner.

One hour later three men were trying to load the horse.

The biggest of the men was in the trailer, pulling on the halter shank. Another man had a rope tied to one side of the trailer. It passed behind the horse, through a ring in the front of the trailer, and back to him as he stood outside the trailer. He pulled on the rope.

The third helper stood behind the gelding and whipped him violently.

The horse was sitting on the butt rope, his front legs braced under the back of the trailer. He had hit his head against the side of the trailer and his right eye was swollen shut. Shortly after, he began to kick.

Scenes like this are absolutely unwarranted, yet they happen all too often.

Too many horse owners neglect to train their horses to load and unload. Instead, they bring the horse to the trailer and try to coax him in with feed and crunchies or they fight with the horse until he gets in.

There are obvious reasons a horse may refuse to load in a trailer. Since a horse's instinct dictates that he never be closed in, that he always be able to run away from danger, and that he always be sure of his footing, a horse trailer is a definite threat to the horse's survival. The trailer is a confined area with a hollow, moving floor. It is a place out of which a horse cannot run when he senses danger.

Pulling or pushing a horse into the trailer will only reinforce his fears. The object in training the horse to load is to lead him to believe that stepping into that trailer was his idea. This is accomplished, not by somehow forcing the horse into the trailer, but by simply bothering him until he decides that being inside the trailer is more comfortable than standing at the back of it.

To train your horse to load, you will need a two-meter (about six feet) stock whip and a halter with a two-meter shank.

Holding the coiled lead shank in your left hand and the whip in your right hand, lead the horse to the back of the trailer.

As the horse reaches the trailer, face his left shoulder and begin to tap him with the whip at the point of the buttocks. Do not whip the horse violently. If you do, he will feel trapped between the whip and the trailer and will try to escape.

Prepare your horse for trailer loading by teaching him to move forward and around you as you direct his head with one hand on the shank and softly tap him on the hindquarters with the whip in your other hand.

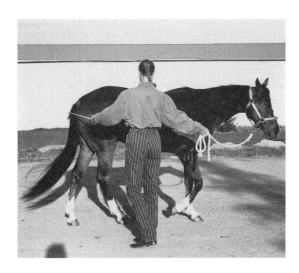

Use the lead rope loosely and only to guide the horse's head toward the trailer.

If your horse becomes anxious at the back of the trailer, lead him away from you into a small circle to the right. This will allow him to relax. After he has made a few circles of three to four meters in diameter immediately behind the trailer, lead him up to the trailer again.

If the horse stops as he gets to the trailer, tap him with the whip. Keep it up until he walks on into the trailer.

Dispense with the tapping as soon as your horse steps into the trailer, even if only one front foot is inside. Your timing is very important at this point. If you continue tapping as he walks on into the trailer, you are punishing him for responding to what you want.

If your horse has both front feet in the trailer but has stopped before he is fully loaded, continue tapping until he steps in with the hind feet.

Never try to force your horse to stay in the trailer. He has to make up his own mind that this is a comfortable place to be. If he backs out at any time, let him do so, but resume tapping on the point of the buttocks as soon as he is out of the trailer.

When your horse is fully loaded and willingly stands in the trailer, let him stand there for a few minutes. Some feed in the trailer will serve as an extra reward for loading.

To train a horse to unload out of a two-horse trailer, be sure to first untie the halter and the butt bar. Run the lead rope between the wall of the trailer and the horse. Standing to the side of the horse's path, apply intermittent pressure on the lead rope and on his tail.

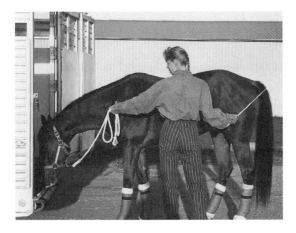

When your horse routinely walks a small circle around you as you direct his head and tap him on the croup, he is ready for the trailer. Bring him up to the trailer and let him stand there until he is comfortable. Once he is relaxed, has looked at and smelled the trailer, face his left shoulder, direct his head into the trailer with your left hand on the shank, and tap him on the croup with the whip in your right hand.

Continue tapping until the horse takes a step forward. As he does, stop tapping. He may be somewhat timid, stepping into the trailer and immediately stepping out again. This is fine. Do not get anxious and tap hard. Doing so will only cause him to fear the trailer. Resume tapping as he stops backing, again directing his head into the trailer. Do not pull on the lead rope. With correct timing as you tap and stop, your horse will learn that it is more comfortable to move forward and into the trailer than to stand outside the trailer.

Eventually, you can discontinue pulling on the lead rope because the horse will recognize a tug on his tail as the cue for unloading.

Plan on spending forty-five minutes to an hour to train your horse to load following this method. If your horse has been spoiled, the process may take longer.

Load and unload your horse several times in one session, repeating the sequence until he walks into the trailer without slowing down or stopping.

In these days of fancy rigs and four-lane highways, it is imperative that all horses load easily. A few hours spent training your horse to load will spare you and him from a lot of headaches down the road.

SADDLING AND BRIDLING

Saddling and bridling your horse eventually becomes a very familiar process, yet attention to detail is always important. A number of things related to saddling can cause problems for you and your horse during riding. A poorly fitted saddle, dirty saddle pad and cinches, or the mishandling of your horse during bridling can result in injury to him or to you.

The first step in saddling your horse is grooming. Brush his entire body, paying particular attention to the areas where the cinch and saddle pad touch him. Unless you remove all dirt and foreign matter from these areas, your horse may develop saddle sores during the ride.

Check your saddle pad for dirt or foreign matter. Clean it if necessary, then place it on the horse's back, halfway up the withers. Then slide the saddle pad back in place, laying down the horse's coat in the process.

Softly place the saddle on your horse's back, as softly as you place your hat on your head. Place a hand on the horn and give the saddle a shake until it slips into place on the horse's back. Let the cinches down and be sure they are not twisted. Generally speaking, the saddle is at the right place on the horse when

Grooming serves as a massage for your horse and increases his blood circulation. It is important to groom after riding. Loosening up the coat and allowing the air to reach the skin prevents various skin diseases.

the front cinch falls approximately four inches behind his elbow.

Place your hand under the saddle pad immediately above the withers and lift it into the gullet of the saddle. Standing next to your horse's left front leg, reach under him and bring the cinch up to the left. Tighten the cinch in a slow, gradual fashion until the saddle is sufficiently tight so as not to roll around your horse.

If your saddle features a back cinch, do it up next. Finally, do up the breast collar. Your horse is ready for the bridle.

Stand on the left side of your horse with the bridle over your left arm. Remove the halter from his head and buckle it around his neck. This important safety practice lets you control your horse while you bridle him. Hold the crown piece of the bridle in your right hand while you spread the curb chain away from the bit with your left. Once the curb chain is far enough away from the bit to allow it to slip behind the chin, press your thumb against the horse's bars in the interdental space. As your horse opens his mouth, pull up on the bridle with your right hand until the mouthpiece meets the corner of the horse's lips. Place the far ear, in this case the right ear, under the crown piece, then place the left ear under the crown piece. Placing the far ear first allows for ease of handling since the headstall is still fairly loose. By the time one ear has been placed through, the headstall is tighter, which makes handling the other ear more difficult.

Place the saddle on your horse softly. Walk around him and lower the cinch.

Tighten the cinch gently and sufficiently for the saddle to stay on the horse. Walk the horse eight or ten strides, then tighten the cinch again, tight enough that you can ride safely.

Be sure the cinch is not twisted before tightening it on your horse.

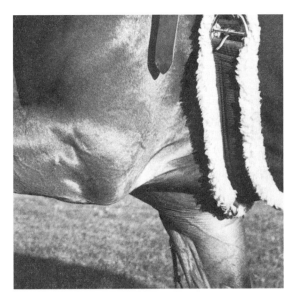

Holding the horse's front leg at the knee, pull it up and forward to stretch the skin from under the cinch to prevent any pinching and blistering.

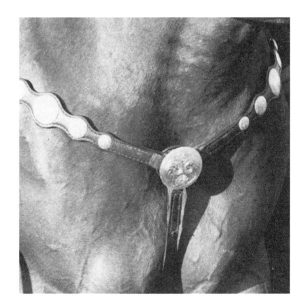

Adjust the breast collar so that the center piece is directly below the neck and in the center of the chest. You should be able to slide your hand between the leather and your horse's chest and shoulders. If the breast collar wrinkles your horse's skin, it is definitely too tight and will cause injury unless readjusted.

Holding the cheek pieces of the headstall together on the bridge of the horse's nose helps control his head during bridling. Note how the rider's left hand separates the curb chain and mouthpiece while her thumb presses on the bars to open the horse's mouth.

Always untie the lead shank and tie the halter around your horse's neck when preparing to bridle your horse.

When passing the headstall over your horse's ears, pass it over the far ear first, then over the closest, usually the left, ear. Be careful to press at the bottom of the ear to fit it under the headstall. The ear is a sensitive part of the horse's anatomy. Bending it in the middle hurts the horse and can make him difficult to bridle.

To mount your horse, face him on the left side. Place your left foot in the stirrup, no deeper than the ball of your foot. Place your right hand on the horn. Hold the reins in your left hand and place it on the horse's neck, six to eight inches ahead of the saddle. Re-main close to your horse's center of gravity as you push yourself up with your left leg.

Before taking the saddle off your horse, tie the cinches and breast collar up to the saddle. This practice pre-vents debris from collecting in the cinch and causing subsequent injuries to your horse.

Once standing in the left stirrup, lean forward over your horse's center of gravity and swing your right leg over your horse's croup, being careful not to bump him with it.

Many horses are made difficult to bridle because riders are careless about the way they handle their horses's ears while bridling and unbridling. The ears are very sensitive. Be sure never to fold a horse's ear in the middle. Rather, push at the base of the ear and lay the entire ear down on the horse's forehead in order to slip the crown piece over the ear.

To remove the bridle, slip it very slowly off the horse's ears and let it down in front of his forehead until the mouthpiece is almost all the way down the interdental space. Hold the bridle in this position for a moment until your horse opens his mouth. When he does, let the bridle down until the mouthpiece is out of his mouth. If your horse does not open his mouth, press with your thumb in the interdental space, just as you did to bridle up. Take as much time as you need to remove the bridle from your horse's head without hitting his teeth with the bit. Ripping the bridle off the horse's head is another way riders make their horses difficult to bridle.

PART II

It takes feel to practice any sport. Feel for the baseball when you get ready to deliver a pitch. Or feel for the golf club handle when you step up for tee-off. It takes feel of many muscles and joints in your body to make that basket count. In horsemanship, it takes feel not only of your own body but also that of your horse. In this part of the book, I show you how to use your mind to develop feel for yourself and for your horse.

Although virtually all riders have heard or read about the seat bones, few know exactly what they look like. I describe the anatomy of the rider and show how different parts of the seat and thighs can hinder or favor your riding, depending on how you use them.

Not only must you be an athlete to be effective at riding various types of horses, but your partner and team member also has his own unique way of moving, his own unique natural abilities, and his own unique disposition. Because you must have balance to move in unity with your horse, I explain how balance is essential to successful horsemanship and detail some sure ways to develop balance.

You can improve your effectiveness and timing on your horse if you are fit and flexible. To this end, I suggest some beneficial exercises you can do with minimal equipment and time.

I show you how you should sit on your horse for best results and explain why your position is important.

Finally, because posting is a useful way to ride the trot, I explain in detail what happens when you post and how to do it correctly.

CHAPTER 3

Rider Psychology

"If you think you can, and if you think you can't, you are right."

—*Henry Ford*

Henry Ford, who is quoted above, was reported to have gone bankrupt three times before the Ford Motor Company finally got off and running. Thomas Edison was an inventor who held more than five hundred patents. To those who asked if he was not discouraged at his failed attempts to invent the light bulb, he responded, "No, every time I fail, it is one more way I know not to build a light bulb." Both of these illustrious men changed the lives of millions of people because of the mental characteristics that were the very essence of their personalities. To these mental characteristics they added learned behavior and technical skills that soon saw them leading in their own field of expertise. In this chapter I discuss some of these mental characteristics, briefly explain how the brain works, and explore a number of mental tools essential to your success as a rider.

RIGHT AND LEFT BRAIN

A basic understanding of the separate functions of the two halves of the human brain will help situate the reader with regard to the way you can use your brain to benefit your riding. Also, a rider needs to identify which side of his or her brain is most dominant and, understanding the role of each half, seek to enhance performance by expanding use of the weaker side.

The brain is made up of a left half and a right half. Each half is characterized by very different functions. The left half is responsible for organized, logical, sequential, step-by-step, rational analysis. It counts, arranges letters into words, and words into sentences, and so on. In riding, the left brain writes down the goals, charts the progress, asks for help on specific aspects of horsemanship, studies the sequence of aids for a particular maneuver, deciphers the proper position needed to achieve a specific exercise, etc. The left brain reads the books, attends clinics, and analyzes videos.

On the other hand, the right brain is the one of intuition, creativity, personal dreams, imagination, and combinations of ideas. It plays a key role in setting and achieving goals as it brainstorms one's dreams. The right brain imagines the goals and sees you actually living them. The right brain gets the idea, then the left brain gets to work and takes the necessary steps. It is your right brain that recalls an event and recognizes the many hundreds of specific feels the horse's motion sends your way as you ride through

Sheldon Soderberg was able to recognize when "Frosty" felt "just right" and cultivate the feeling. That is how the two garnered such an impressive list of awards. AQHA stallion Frosty Zipper is a Superior Western Pleasure horse and World Show qualifier. Frosty Zipper was also QHAA Hi-point Junior Western Pleasure in 1991 and finished the show year Top Ten in the nation.
(Photo: Sharon Latimer)

various maneuvers. It recognizes the feel of your horse as he lopes on the correct or on the wrong lead, or the way your horse stops on his front quarters when the cow is on his left side, or the feel of him leaning into the third barrel.

The sum of your feels make you or break you as a rider. All the "book knowledge" in the world will not make you a successful rider unless you can feel the horse. This is why it is important to ride with the right brain: an all left-brain approach focuses only on the theory of horsemanship and the brain does not have time to sift through all the theory since many things happen at once when you are riding. A developed right brain will accumulate the feels that result from the application of the theory and file them in a sort of memory bank. Think of the memory bank as the hard drive on a computer, and the right brain as the menu through which you can store or retrieve the feels. As you gain more riding experience, applying your right brain to feeling the horse's responses lets you store more feels on your "hard drive." Later, as your horse performs, your right brain recognizes the feels as desirable or undesirable and your body reacts accordingly, by correcting or rewarding the horse, with more accurate and effective aids than ever possible through the reasonable, step-by-step process of the left brain.

However, depending solely on the right brain presents some shortcomings. Riders who make more use of their right brain and less of their left brain can get on a horse and perform wonderful exercises but cannot tell you how they got the horse to do it. In many cases they can barely describe the feel of the execution. They lack the left brain theoretical understanding of the exercise. When they get into a problem with a horse, these riders often cannot get out of it because they do not understand the whys and wherefores of the maneuver. These riders make poor coaches as they cannot communicate the complete picture to their students. Likewise, riders who depend mostly on the left brain's sequential reasoning have difficulties sorting out a horsemanship or horse-training problem because they do not feel the horse's reactions. They understand all the theory about the positioning but do not recognize the horse's responses because they lack depth in their "feel hard drive." You can see by this very brief description of the roles of the two halves of the brain that a balanced use of both is key to the effective rider: understanding the effect of improper positioning on the flying-lead change is important to the rider for example, and being able to feel when the horse has changed leads is equally important.

A most effective way to whole-brain riding is to study the theory of the horse's body position and combinations of aids by reading books, watching videos, attending clinics, etc. and to forget about it while you are riding. Indeed, when riding, simply listen and feel for the horse's reactions and responses. If you are reasoning to yourself about the complicated positioning of the horse and appropriate use of your aids while your horse is moving through a particular maneuver, you are engaged in a left-brain process that will likely take much longer than the time needed for your horse to execute the exercise. As you reason through this step-by-step process, your right brain is unable to store data in the "feel hard drive." So as you school your horse or yourself, think of the way he feels to you rather than focusing on the left-brain step-by-step theory. If you have internalized the theory, you will not have to focus on it and will be able to store or retrieve feels from your "hard drive" and apply the correct aids to your horse.

I have seen the opposite approach many times: the rider tries to deal with a riding difficulty by constantly repeating the theory to him- or herself. During this repetitious recital, the rider's right brain is not listening to the responses and reactions of the horse and not storing any feels. The result is a tense, frustrated rider and a confused horse whose very subtle attempts at responding are not rewarded (because they are not felt) and will soon be abandoned.

Use images to help you recognize the feels you are looking to identify. In her book *Centered Riding*, Sally Swift uses numerous images designed to help the rider develop the correct feel for a particular aspect of riding. I have also used images in this book whenever applicable. Add your own images as well. Talk to other riders and coaches and ask them how they recognize feels, and set your right brain free to let you and your horse work as a team.

PERSONAL ATTRIBUTES OF THE SUCCESSFUL RIDER

A most fundamental requirement of success is accepting responsibility for your own achievements and failures. This principle applies not only to horsemanship, regardless of which equestrian event you practice, but also to all other aspects of your life. If you want something to happen—a change in something you are doing, an improvement in performance, or a betterment of your situation—you must recognize that you are responsibile for making those things happen. Making excuses and blaming the instructor, your horse, or the arena owners for a riding problem, or perhaps the judge for a questionable placing, will never result in improvement of your horsemanship skills. In fact, by blaming others, you place a large portion of the outcome in their hands and rob yourself of the opportunity to change your performance. Blaming is diametrically opposed to taking responsibility and the more you blame others, the less likely you are to take it upon yourself to change your lot.

Once you have taken responsibility for your performance, improvements will not come until you commit yourself to the task. To be committed is defined as devoting oneself unreservedly. Commitment to effective and winning horsemanship often means financial sacrifices so that you can afford the quality coaching necessary to achieving your goals. It may mean that other hobbies are shelved for a while. It may necessitate a change in your eating habits so that you can maintain an effective riding weight. Commitment to effective horsemanship may mean a change in your daily schedule so that you can school your horse and yourself on a regular basis. It may also mean leaving your ego behind and attending horsemanship clinics where instructors can help you with the weaknesses in your performance.

Many riders are talented and well mounted but are not prepared to make the sacrifices necessary to become effective and winning riders. Those who are committed often outshine those who are not.

To accept responsibility for your own success and to commit yourself to it is not all that is required. To succeed, you must work hard and smart.

Working hard and smart means you ride those additional horses on a regular basis so that you can develop a better feel. It means you take every opportunity to listen and learn something new and you try to apply it to yourself or your horse. It means you read all the material that applies to your sport or event. It means you watch videos of yourself riding and recognize those things you do well and those that you need to change, then use proven focusing methods to identify feels and improve your technique.

Consider the example of one of my students. Jane was an average rider with a full-time job

Just as in all other sports, advanced skills, such as those required to spin a horse at a fast speed, come only after a rider has demonstrated commitment through sacrifices, persistence, and effort. (Photo: Ted Gard)

and an average income. Her horse was well schooled but not an exceptional performer. Jane needed to improve her body position and refine the use of her aids to be competitive in the horsemanship class.

To achieve her goal, she rode her horse four to five times a week and also took up schooling a friend's horse so that she could develop more feel for the horse's responses and avoid becoming a one-horse rider. She also took lessons from a qualified coach twice a week and learned how to use focusing techniques to better apply everything she had learned.

Successful riders become so by spending thousands of hours in the saddle and focusing during every minute. That is hard and smart work.

Another important personal characteristic of successful riders is their confidence in themselves and in the schooling of their horses. Self-confidence is an intrinsic belief that you can do whatever you set your mind to.

In 1990, the year he won the NRHA Futurity, Doug Milholland rode Silver Anniversary to within one-half point of the minimum qualifying score for the Finals. This gave Doug and the gray mare the right to ride in the Consolation class, the winner of which may show in the Finals.

The stakes were high, with the winner cashing in on $100,000. Twelve to fourteen months of hard and smart work had gone into each one of the four hundred horses entered into the Futurity. Much depended on Doug's confidence in the schooling he had put into the mare and his assessment of her ability and disposition.

Doug won the Consolation and was the first entry in the Finals. Through the entire pattern he asked Silver Anniversary for all she had and she gave it all. They won the Futurity.

In preparing the mare for the Finals, Doug rode some circles, stopped her a few times, and kept her quiet. He did not turn her around nor did he ask for anything difficult from her. He was confident the mare would respond in the show ring.

A rider may lack self-confidence for several reasons. He or she may be aware of a lack of physical or/and mental preparation. If this is the way you feel before entering the show ring or mounting your horse, then you need to prepare yourself better. You may need to take more lessons, ride your horse more often, and perhaps send him to a trainer. Perhaps you need to embark on a weight-reducing and fitness program. Or perhaps you feel unprepared because you are nervous and not completely in control of all your thoughts. Later in this chapter I describe methods for teaching yourself how to relax. Also helpful in preparing yourself and building self-confidence are the techniques of imagery and focusing, both of which are described in this chapter. Take time to read carefully and practice them at home before you get on your horse; then practice them on horseback and see how much more prepared you feel next time you ride in the show ring.

Self-confidence comes from making informed choices about your horsemanship and the schooling of your horse. It comes from achieving realistic goals; small ones to begin with, then more challenging ones, such as a regional final or a national championship. I'll talk more about goal setting later in this chapter.

Persistence is another important characteristic of the successful rider. It means to continue firmly despite opposition and difficulties until a goal is achieved.

Classic Ryan is an Appaloosa stallion I trained as a reining and working cow horse. Ryan was an athletic horse with strong circles and fast flat spins. His lead changes were very smooth and correct. His sliding stops, although long and soft, were not so natural for him. It took a great deal of preparation and work on the basic suppling and body-control exercises to get him to the point where he learned to slide on a consistent basis. Persistence paid off as he went on to earn several reining and working cow horse points.

Persistence also pays off when you work on your riding skills. Three to four months of work on the lunge line performing the exercises described in chapter 4 can greatly improve your balance, seat, and effectiveness, even if there are days when you seem to be getting nowhere.

SETTING GOALS

Setting goals is paramount to successful horsemanship. In his book *The 7 Habits of Highly Effective People*, Stephen Covey says of goals:

> *An effective goal focuses primarily on results rather than activity. It identifies where you want to be and, in the process, helps you determine where you are. It gives you important information on how to get there, and it tells you when you have arrived. It unifies your efforts and energy. It gives meaning and purpose to all you do. And it can finally translate itself into daily activities so that you are pro-active, you are in charge of your life, you are making happen each day the things that will enable you to fulfil your personal mission statement.*

Covey speaks of goals in terms of helping us achieve our personal mission, the most encompassing of all our goals.

Without goals riders often become simple passengers on their horses' backs. They ride from day to day but never really improve. They settle on a plateau, always running into the same problems on different horses, perhaps changing bits or using other tricks to solve the problems, or even selling the horse and finding another one. Setting goals would help those riders and bring them to higher levels of accomplishment and enjoyment.

Goal setting has much to do with establishing self-confidence, for constant failure to reach established goals destroys one's belief in his or her capability to achieve any goal. On the other hand, an achieved goal, no matter how small, is a great confidence builder and can send the rider forward to conquer the next challenge. For this reason you need to break long-term, high goals into several more attainable short-term ones. Just as climbing a stairway is usually done one step at a time, so should long-term goals be paced.

Long-term goals can include qualifying for a specific competition or being able to ride a certain pattern at a designated speed. Or a long-term goal could be rider related, such as being able to ride in balance without reins and stirrups at all three gaits. Short-term goals could include such things as minimum number of riding hours each week, an amount of time spent riding without stirrups during each session, specific skills to have attained in one month, two months, etc.

Frustrated riders have given up on setting goals because they never seem to reach them or even improve if they do reach them. In talking with such riders I have often discovered that their goals were something like "Win the World Championship five years from now." While this is a very respectable goal, these riders are usually very vague when I ask what they are going to do today, tomorrow, and the day after that will take them to their long-term goal. And the fact that they have not defined these short-term goals very specifically in their minds is the reason they have not reached the long-term goals they set for themselves. Therefore, once you have set a long-term goal, answer for yourself the question "What will I do during the next half-hour, half-day, week, two weeks, month, six months, year that will help me reach this long-term goal?"

All the literature on goal setting agrees that, to be effective, goals must feature five characteristics. They must be specific, measurable, action oriented, realistic, and timeable. Use the acronym SMART to check the validity of your goals. For instance, a goal that states "I want to ride well" is not very specific or timeable. A much more SMART goal reads "I will prepare and show my horse in the Non-pro Reining at the State Fair Horse Show in August." This goal is certainly specific, since it indicates the class entered and the location of the show. It is measurable in the sense that the rider will either show or not show his or her horse. The aspect of measurement is very important to the realization of our goals; that which we can measure we tend to do much more than that which we cannot measure. The goal is action oriented since it makes use of the action verbs *prepare* and *show*. The goal "I would like to ride my horse" is not action oriented and will likely get dropped for the first excuse that presents itself.

Several factors must be considered to determine whether a goal is realistic for you. You will need to answer many questions, such as how much time can you spend riding your horse and practicing? How much money can you spend on lessons and training for your horse? What about your horse's age, his disposition and ability? Is he able to take you to your goal? How about facilities? Can you ride when the weather is cold or wet, or will bad weather slow down your progress? If you are not sure what may be a realistic goal for you, you may need to enlist the help of an experienced coach who is familiar with your situation. Join groups or associate with people who have the same goals you have. Or find someone who has achieved the same goals you set for yourself and ask all the specific how-to questions. Too often riders are not familiar enough with the implications of achieving the goals they set for themselves. So many times I have seen riders set for themselves a goal to perform a Western Riding pattern within weeks, not realizing that they were still two years away from being able to bring their horses to perform a balanced, correct flying-lead change, much less seven of them separated by only a few strides.

Finally, a goal must be timeable. If you do not put a time limit on your goals, you are not likely to achieve them, and even if you do, determining that you have will be difficult.

An example of a SMART goal for an intermediate rider who wants to develop balance may be "I will perform exercises on horseback, while being lunged, for fifteen minutes a day until I can do all exercises at all three gaits, with my eyes closed."

An important aspect of attaining goals is to write them down when you set them. Writing your goals forces you to think about them in a specific manner and ensures that you will not forget or confuse them. Writing your goals also serves as a sort of contract with yourself and is in itself a motivator to achievement. Don't worry about not achieving your goals and being reminded of it if you wrote them down. You can always change your goals if they were not realistic. What seemed realistic ten or twelve months ago may no longer be suitable to your situation: you may have moved, been forced to

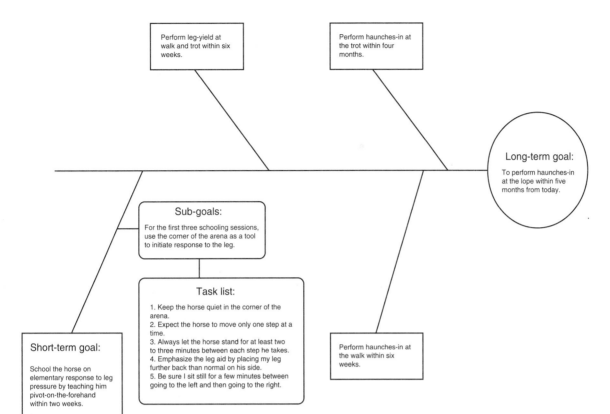

Perform leg-yield at walk and trot within six weeks.

Perform haunches-in at the trot within four months.

Long-term goal:

To perform haunches-in at the lope within five months from today.

Sub-goals:

For the first three schooling sessions, use the corner of the arena as a tool to initiate response to the leg.

Task list:

1. Keep the horse quiet in the corner of the arena.
2. Expect the horse to move only one step at a time.
3. Always let the horse stand for at least two to three minutes between each step he takes.
4. Emphasize the leg aid by placing my leg further back than normal on his side.
5. Be sure I sit still for a few minutes between going to the left and then going to the right.

Short-term goal:

School the horse on elementary response to leg pressure by teaching him pivot-on-the-forehand within two weeks.

Perform haunches-in at the walk within six weeks.

This diagram shows a logical and sequential method of writing down your goals. Goals are in chronological order from left to right. Short-term goals are in the rectangles. Sub-goals and task lists are in the rounded corner boxes. Each short-term goal should have sub-goals and a task list.

sell your horse, you may have sustained an injury, and so forth. If your goals are written down, you have a record of the unattainable goal and it can serve as a lesson for the future.

After you have set long- and short-term goals, you need to further divide them into sub-goals. Sub-goals should also be SMART—if they are, they too are more likely to be achieved. Let's go through an example of long-term, short-term, and sub-goals for a rider wishing to develop hindquarter control in her the horse.

You need to know where you want to end up before you can pinpoint the steps to get there. Begin by setting your long-term goal. In this instance, your long-term goal may read this way: to perform haunches-in (move the horse's hindquarters to the left and then to the right of the line of travel) at the walk, trot, and lope within five months from today.

Your short-term goals may be: (1) School the horse on elementary response to leg pressure by teaching him pivot on the forehand within two weeks. (2) Perform leg-yield at the walk and trot within six weeks. (3) Perform haunches-in at the walk within six weeks. (4) Perform haunches-in at the trot within four months.

You may further break down your short-term goals into sub-goals. Sub-goals for your first short-term goal may read: (1) For the first three schooling sessions, use the corner of the riding arena as a tool to initiate response to the leg. (2) Remove my aids and give the horse a rest after each quarter of turns for the first two weeks.

To help ensure the achievement of your goals, write a task list for each short-term goal. A task list includes all the components of a short-term goal. Writing one forces you to study a maneuver and lets you think of all the details you must consider when you school your horse on that particular maneuver. To make a task list really worth the effort, take the time to develop it; make a project of discussing all of its different aspects with an experienced coach. Read about the maneuver in various periodicals and watch videotapes on the topic. Summarize the information, then write your task list. A task list for a sub-goal might read: (1) Keep the horse quiet in the corner of the arena. (2) Expect the horse to move only one step at a time. (3) Always let the horse stand for at least two to three minutes between each step he takes. (4) Emphasize the leg aid by placing my leg farther back than normal on his side. (5) Be sure to sit still for a few minutes between going to the left and then going to the right.

If you are not sure you can remember all the elements of your task list, carry it in your pocket while you ride. There is no sense researching a maneuver and then forgetting to apply the knowledge gained, on the horse, at the appropriate time.

A final but important word regarding goal setting: Your goals should be personal performance goals rather than outcome goals. An example of an outcome goal is "Win this particular event" or "Place ahead of this particular rider." Such outcome goals place all the emphasis on winning and, since you have little control of the goals of others, you place yourself under much anxiety. This anxiety often hinders the performance instead of enhancing it. Much more conducive to the development of excellence—and eventually winning—is the setting of personal performance goals, or skills goals, based on the principle that success is attaining your own goals rather than somehow surpassing the goals of others.

Now that you understand how to set goals, let's look at three skills important to the achievement of goals: focusing, imagery, and self-talk.

FOCUSING

The focusing process makes possible the elimination of the distractions that clutter your mind and interfere with thoughts that are important to the realization of your goals. Spectators, kids throwing pop cans, the wind in the fairground flags, someone bathing a horse, etc. are all activities and thoughts that are not relevant to your ride and can be considered as meaningless stimuli. The more you can tune out meaningless stimuli and think only of things that are important to your ride, the more successful you will be. Focusing will help you reach a higher degree of consciousness and, by bringing your goals to

the forefront of your mind, you will avoid the plateaus often experienced by those who do not use the process. Later I describe the three steps to focusing and outline a focusing practice. But first, let's look at how we can block out meaningless stimuli.

Although this is easier said than done, it is very important for you to be able to clear your mind of all unrelated thoughts before you even catch your horse. A bad day at the office or a difficult ride earlier on another horse can easily turn you into an ineffective, reactive, and destructive rider. To prevent other concerns from disrupting your ride, do not think of the nonrelated topic as you mount your horse. Rather, set a short-term goal for yourself for the moment you get on your horse. Something like this: Perform ten repetitions of each horseback exercise within the first ten minutes of the ride. Then go about achieving this goal immediately. Usually, once you have attained this very short-term goal, your mind is focused on the ride and the other unimportant thoughts are dissipated.

You need not be sitting on your horse, however, to practice blocking out meaningless stimuli. In fact, you can practice blocking out stimuli whenever you find yourself in a noisy, busy, or intimidating environment. And the more often you practice, the more effective you will be when you get on your horse.

Perhaps the setting in which you are reading this book is a good place to start. Locate a picture on a wall of the room. Find a specific object in the picture and focus on it. Do not think of anything else, but rather analyse everything about the object. Then focus on a very small part of the object, such as a ray of light on a photograph or a trace of dust on the frame. Hold the focus for as long as you can, then try again, using a different object. Practice this focusing technique in various locations with increasing levels of noise and visual distractions.

An important aspect of focusing in the equestrian sport is the fact that a rider's focus must constantly vary between broad and narrow. The focus is narrow when the rider thinks only of herself and her horse. It becomes broad when the rider has to locate herself in the arena in order to guide her horse to the third barrel or among the other competitors. This type of broad-to-narrow-and-broad-again focusing demands practice. Obviously, the rider focusing broadly does not want to take in all of the activities on the show grounds. Rather, the focus is only on the riding space and the possible objects within it, such as barrels, poles, a herd and a cow in front of the horse, or trail obstacles.

An effective way to practice this particular mode of focusing is to stand at the entrance of a riding arena and focus on a particular hoofprint in the sand in the middle of the arena, then take in the entire riding surface with a less intense focus, then again focus on the hoofprint, and so on. Practice the broad-to-narrow technique while riding your horse in familiar surroundings, then in foreign environments.

As a first step to focusing, assess the environment in which you find yourself while in need of focus. This assessment is important because it allows you to block out of your mind those things that are meaningless to your performance. It is important to notice all the details that might possibly distract you as you ride: the dog tied to the gatepost, the kids running around the concession stand, the location of the exit gate to which your horse may be drawn, the flags flapping in the wind, etc. You cannot afford surprises. You also need to assess how your ride feels and how your horse is responding: Does he feel fresh, perhaps too energetic, or sluggish and too laid back? Is he moving away from the outside rein as he should be or as well as he does at home? Once you have gathered all this information and categorized what is important and what is irrelevant, you are ready to go on to the next step in focusing, which is analysis of the information.

This analysis is very important to focusing because it allows you to develop a plan of action, with very specific details, on which you will then act. For instance, if you found your horse to be a touch sluggish and difficult to keep balanced, you might decide to use more leg and seat aids and not ride him as much as you usually do. In particular, you would plan to use more driving aids in that small circle you know you have to ride. In addition, you may have found,

during the assessment process, that your horse tends to fall out of the circle when he nears the exit gate. Therefore, you will resolve to use more outside leg and outside rein as you near that point in the circle.

Perhaps the analysis has more to do with you than with your horse. You may have found yourself somewhat nervous and consequently stiff in the midsection. A conclusion of your analysis then may be that you will indulge in positive self-talk (more on this later) until you are actually riding in the ring. Your analysis is based on your past experiences and your knowledge of the sport: The more experience and know-how you possess, the more detailed the analysis will be.

The third step in focusing is the actual carrying out of the plan. This is when you carry out the plan decided upon in your analysis. And with your ability to tune out meaningless stimuli, you should have no problem applying your leg aids at the right time or keeping the other competitors from psyching you out of the game. The results should be that you can ride your horse anywhere and be able to totally block out the other riders, the crowd, your relatives, the judge, and so forth. You are aware of just you and your horse, as if there were nothing else in the world. Once you are able to tune out meaningless stimuli, you are ready to develop a plan upon which you can focus.

IMAGERY

Imagery is the application of your imagination to the achievement of your goals. It is based on the fact that "experimental and clinical psychologists have proved beyond the shadow of a doubt that the human nervous system cannot tell the difference between an 'actual' experience and an experience imagined vividly and in detail." (Maxwell Maltz, M.D., F.I.C.S., *Psycho-Cybernetics* [Englewood Cliffs: Prentice Hall]) In the same book, Dr. Maltz goes on to say: "the so-called 'subconscious mind' is not a mind after all, but a mechanism—a goal striving, 'servo-mechanism' consisting of the brain and nervous system, which is *used by* and *directed by* the mind. The latest and most usable concept is that man does not have two minds but a mind or consciousness, which operates an automatic, goal striving machine." Further, according to Maltz, the subconscious mind strives to achieve those goals which are most clearly defined by mental images.

This is the reason for the great benefits of mastering the art of imagery: Often visualizing yourself achieving your goals defines them as mental images and then your subconscious/goal-striving mechanism has the potential to guide your actions toward the accomplishment of the image. In an experiment with a basketball team, players who were kept off the court and practiced baskets through imagery were found to be as accurate and successful as those who were practicing on the court for the same period of time. Detailed imaginary repetitions of a reining or equitation pattern is akin to your riding your horse through the pattern, in front of the judge, wearing your show clothes—for as many times as you imagine yourself doing it. When repeated often enough, riding the perfect pattern becomes a habit, and even if you have actually only ridden the pattern twice on horseback, your subconscious mind takes over and your body acts out of memory. Imagery makes it possible for you to practice the same skill over and over until you have mastered all the elements.

To open and close a gate correctly you must first be able to see yourself doing it in your mind's eye. This important process is called imagery. If you can not imagine yourself doing it, you probably will not be able to do it well.

With imagery, your practice time is not limited to your or your horse's level of fitness: you can keep on training even if one of you is laid up.

Effective imagery is possible only when you are physically and mentally relaxed. Only then can you focus your senses enough to define a clear picture for your subconscious.

To teach yourself to relax, find a quiet place where you can sit down comfortably or even lie down. Clear your mind of all thoughts except those of your body. Close your eyes and, beginning with your feet, tense the muscles of the toes, feet, and ankles. Feel the muscles as they become increasingly tighter. Hold them tight for five seconds, then release the tension. After you have released the tension, feel how heavy your feet are. Repeat the process one more time, then work on the muscles of your calves, then your thighs, and so on, all the way to your head and facial muscles. When your entire body feels very heavy and limp, you are ready to imagine yourself riding your goals.

Beneficial imagery demands commitment and some practice since it requires the use of all the senses to set the stage as it will be when you perform your goal. At this time, see yourself ride your horse. Include pictures of the riding arena, the judge in his stand. See yourself in your riding clothes. See the colors of the flags and the sponsors' advertising signs. Hear the noise typical of the surroundings, see your horse's neck and the saddle horn and swells in front of you. Imagine the feel of the saddle in your seat and thighs, the weight of your legs in the stirrups, the horse's mouth as he gives to the contact of the bit. Imagine the specific feelings your horse sends your way as you prepare him for each and every maneuver you execute. Feel him as he bends and takes that turn around the barrel. Or feel him as he locks on to that cow and stops hard to cut her off to the left. Feel his shoulders move as he executes that turn on the haunches. Concentrate on your horse's movements, balance, and his responsiveness. Build in the detailed application of all your aids, your facial expressions, etc. Then imagine yourself, with all the details again, passing the test with high marks and receiving the certificate. Or see yourself winning the big class and proudly standing with the trophy, your friends, and family for the photo session.

Remember, imaging is mapping your subconscious so that you can depend on it later; therefore, practice exercises and maneuvers the correct way. Be sure your horse responds to your aids correctly and at the right time in your mind. Watch a rider you want to emulate, file the image into your memory, then incorporate that image into your detailed image. Picture yourself riding like this person and your central nervous system will take over. Your muscles will act out of memory. For instance, do you have a problem with moving your hands too fast? Watch someone who has the sort of hand aids you want to adopt, then imagine yourself moving your hands the same way. Spend twenty minutes to a half-hour a day visualizing yourself in this exercise, and your hands will begin to slow down.

Imaging helps you locate the areas of your goals to which you need to pay more attention. For instance, you are not concentrating enough if imagining riding a particular pattern takes longer than the time allowed for it in the horse show. It is important to practice thinking as fast as will be necessary in the horse show: A trail class pattern may allow for only three loping strides before you have to stop and sidepass over a rail. If you gear your mind to think about loping for two minutes, you will be surprised and caught unprepared at the show. Should the way your horse feels to you and his performance in a particular maneuver not be very clear in your mind, then either you or your horse are not ready to define the goal clearly in your subconscious mind and probably will fall short on that maneuver during the actual riding. In this case, get more instruction and practice time until you master the skill and can focus the image.

Practice the relaxing and imagery techniques as often as possible. The more you practice them, the more coordinated you will become and the more effective you will be under stress situations such as tests and horse shows.

SELF-TALK

At the beginning of the section on imagery I discussed the subconscious or goal-striving mechanism as something of an automatic pilot system that attempts to achieve the goals most clearly defined as mental pictures in your mind. Dr Maltz states that this combination of your "conscious mind and your goal-striving mechanism" leads to success or failure, depending on the thoughts you entertain. It is important to understand that the goal-striving mechanism of your subconscious mind does not select the mental image it strives for. It does not reason as to whether the image it is striving for is one of success or failure. It simply goes for the most clearly defined goal. Therefore, the responsibility to determine which mental image the subconscious will strive to attain rests with the conscious mind.

This has very clear implications: The type of thoughts you entertain will clarify a mental picture and therefore orient your goal-striving mechanism. If you focus on your desire to ride at a specific upper level, your goal-striving mechanism will strive for it. If you focus on your shortcomings, the image will be one of failure and your goal-striving mechanism will lead you to more failures. The result is low self-esteem, marked by a belief that you cannot achieve the goals you tentatively set for yourself. This low self-esteem leads to more negative thoughts and the cycle of negativity continues.

Therefore, instead of entertaining thoughts of how poorly you sit when your horse turns the first barrel, think of, and repeat out loud to yourself, how you will sit next time you ride your horse around that barrel. In other words, instead of focusing on your weaknesses, focus on the actions needed to overcome them.

Effective and successful people have learned to see the praiseworthy side of other people and things, the side that builds them and others up rather than that which tears down, depresses, and frustrates. They do not see a partly cloudy sky, but rather one that is partly sunny. Listen to yourself think and talk of your performance; do you see the partly sunny sky or the partly cloudy one? Are you seeing and talking of yourself as not able to sit a sliding stop, or are you thinking in positive terms such as, "My ability to sit a sliding stop is improving." You see, much of the improvement in your ability to sit the sliding stop, or do anything else, is directly linked to whether you see the clouds, or whether you see the sun: if you do not believe your ability is improving, it will not improve.

A restrictive left brain is one of the biggest barriers to success. Too many riders allow their left brain to set boundaries to the imagination and dreams of their right brain. Their left hemisphere says, "No way, you can't do that. Look at how little you know, or how unathletic you are. You go and try this and you will be the laughing stock of the other riders." This kind of boundary setting self-talk is possibly the most common reason a great mass of people settle for a lesser degree of achievement than what they could have attained.

Positive self-talk does not mean that you should never think of the negative experiences of the past. Those experiences carry several lessons essential to your future success. To benefit from such experiences, draw the lessons from them and forget about the details. For to dwell on these events defines the images of failure and gives your subconscious a license to strive for more failures. For instance, if you lost an equitation class because your horse did not back up correctly, analyze the situation in a step-by-step fashion to determine what went wrong, then forget about the fact that you lost the class. Rather, think only of the solutions you decided to implement as a result of the step-by-step analysis.

If you find yourself using negative words, you need to make a conscious effort to eliminate them from your vocabulary. In her book *That Winning Feeling*, Jane Savoie provides a list of negative sentences riders use and suggests a positive substitute for each one (p. 34). Savoie also suggests eliminating from your vocabulary the words *try, depressed, discouraged,* and *frustrated,* and replacing the word *if* with the much more affirmative *when.*

In addition to self-talk, a most profound way to build a positive self-image is to volunteer to help others when you are able. Devoting yourself to the help and success of others builds respect for others and a recognition that people are important to your life. This recognition puts all aspects of horsemanship into perspective and counter-balances the pressures and frustrations you may sometimes experience with your own riding. As a result, you will acquire much self-confidence as you watch others benefit from your knowledge, and you will learn so much more about horsemanship in the process of instructing. A word of caution: Do not offer advice unless it is requested. Too many riders are not tactful in the way they share knowledge, and consequently destroy potentially enriching relationships with riding peers.

The environment in which you ride can have a great influence on the type of self-talk you entertain. Learn to tune out people who are too often negative and complaining. Do not listen to them blame others for their problems. Their derogatory comments are like a disease of the mind and they undermine your goal-striving, proactive efforts.

PREPARING FOR THE TEST OR SHOW RING

You have put in countless focused hours on horseback. You sacrificed other activities so that you could fit your lessons into your coach's busy schedule. You read the sections on rider psychology and practiced relaxation techniques over and over again to the point at which all you have to do is think about the relaxation routine to feel the tension leave your body. You researched your goals and, in consultation with your coach, wrote them down in a detailed format. You are a positive individual who uses imagery as a way to develop your riding skills. You have applied all these techniques to your daily practice sessions and have become a better rider as a result.

Things are different, however, the day of the show or test. Clearly, the mental preparation described earlier will greatly reduce the stress level. Nevertheless, the day of the show you can take some practical steps to further eliminate stress.

Arrive at the show early so that you do not feel rushed to get yourself and your horse ready. Feeling rushed for fear of missing the class is a sure way to raise your level of tension above the effective stage. Your aids become abrupt and unusually erratic and your otherwise well-schooled horse becomes upset and confused. Arriving at the show well ahead of time also gives you time to survey the environment and go through the focusing process described earlier.

As you groom and tack your horse, go through the same routine you use at home. This is important not only for your horse but also for you: Routines give you a sense of comfort and mastery. As you ride to the warmup ring, make sure you have set a very specific goal, as many riders lose their class or test in the warmup ring. That is, they win the warmup but have little left to show in the actual class. Their anxiety overtakes them and they change the schooling routine upon which they have built for the last several months. A specific goal, tailored to you and your horse, will prevent your show nerves from taking over when you see a fellow competitor perform blazing maneuvers in the warmup ring.

Take the opportunity to ride your horse in the actual show ring during intermissions. As you ride in the show arena, practice the broad-to-narrow-to-broad-again focusing in preparation for tuning out the spectators, announcer stand, etc. If your contest requires that you ride a pattern, stop at the end of the arena and locate the center of the riding surface. Determine the location of the markers and the judge's stand and imagine yourself riding the pattern several times as you practice tuning out everyone else in the ring.

Have your chaps and your number ready well ahead of time so that you do not have to run back to the barn and get them at the last minute. Avoid unnecessary talking with anyone for the last thirty minutes before your class. This period of time is critical to your focusing on your ride and imagining yourself showing your horse. Any visiting with friends, relatives, or

Studying the rules and patterns is an important part of preparing for the show.

fellow competitors will only serve to distract you from the important job at hand. There will be plenty of time for friendly conversations after the class.

All through the hours before the class, listen to yourself and respond to any nervousness or negativity by applying the now-familiar relaxation, focusing, self-talk, and imagery techniques you practiced at home.

As you enter the ring, remind yourself of your goals for this ride, and say to yourself, "I know I can do it." Deep, smooth breaths from the stomach help your midsection and seat muscles relax and settle you deep in the saddle. Smiling also relaxes you and adds to your positive self-talk. Besides, a smiling countenance facilitates blood flow to the brain, an important aspect of effective riding, considering that blood carries oxygen to the cells. Finally, correct posture as you ride into the ring could make or break your ride. Not only could the judge mark you down, but correct posture—shoulders up and broad, chest out, and back flat—relaxes your midsection and neck, and facilitates blood flow and breathing.

As you ride your class, maintain a positive approach. If a particular section of the class does not feel just right, do not fall into a negative thinking process by feeling disappointment or even shame. Remember, there is more of the class to ride and you need to think ahead of your horse to the maneuvers you still need to perform, not spend time thinking about the ones you have done already. Telling yourself that you should have been better prepared only leads to confusion and failure. Look ahead to attaining the remainder of your goal.

After the class, congratulate the other competitors. This friendly gesture is often missing in the show arena yet it is a most important step to keeping goals in perspective. Respecting other competitors and openly congratulating them for their success helps you separate the people aspect of the show arena from your technical goals. By doing so, you will keep focusing on improving your goals rather than trying to better someone else's goals. Several hours after the contest, think about what went right and what can be improved upon. Adjust your schooling program if necessary, or perhaps even adjust your goals. And remember: As long as you are aware of why you experienced specific difficulties and find out how to go about correcting them, you are winning, regardless of your placing in the class.

The Independent Seat

The independent seat is fundamental to successful horse-manship.

One of your foremost riding goals—no matter what event you wish to specialize in—should be to develop an independent seat. In this chapter I explain why an independent seat is important and how to achieve this most basic yet fundamental state of body and mind. I begin with a description of the important parts of the rider's seat.

ANATOMY OF THE SEAT

Knowledge of your own anatomy is key to being an effective rider. This knowledge results in an increased body awareness. When you have a clear picture of the shape of the pelvis, the exact location of what are commonly called seat bones, and their relationship to the other parts of your midsection, you can better understand the various applications of the seat bones. Knowing the rider's anatomy makes it possible for the coach to communicate to the learner the reasons why certain positions or actions of the body work or do not work. For the purpose of horsemanship, we will study the pelvis, the thighbone, the hip joint, the muscles of the thigh, the abdominal muscles, and the back muscles.

The Pelvis

The pelvis is a solid ring of bones composed of two halves joined at the front of the pubic crest. You can feel your pubic crest by pressing with your fingers at the lower end of your abdomen. From the pubic crest, the two halves develop into the ascending pubic ramus, the descending pubic ramus, the ischial ramus, and the ischial tuberosity. Squat and feel with your hands the rearmost part of your seat bones (ischial tuberosity). Now follow the bony ridges toward the front (ischial ramus). Two and one-half to three inches from the rearmost point, the seat bones bend up toward the pelvis (descending pubic ramus). That section of bone between the ischial tuberosity and the descending pubic ramus forms the base of support for the rider's body. Immediately above the ischial tuberosity is the ischium, above which we find the hip socket. Above the hip socket is the seemingly carved-out ilium, crowned by the iliac crest. The iliac crest is the bony ridge you feel when you place your hands on your hips. Finally, the two halves are joined at the rear by the solid bottom part of the spine called the sacrum. This joint of the pelvis and the sacrum is called the sacroiliac joint. It is a solid joint, which means that every time the lower back hollows out, or rounds out, the sacrum and pelvis tip forward or back, respectively. This fact is important to note; its implications are discussed later as we talk about balance and position.

The Thigh

Turning our attention to the femur, or thigh-bone, we note four parts of interest: the head, the neck, the greater trochanter, and the body. The head is covered with cartilage and fits into the hip socket. The neck, in the adult of average size, extends about one to two inches in length. This length of the neck places the femur away from the pelvis, permitting more leverage from certain muscles and greater flexibility of the hip joint. The greater trochanter is a broad flat process at the upper end of the lateral surface of the thighbone, to which several muscles are attached. You can feel your trochanter by placing your hands on the side of your thighs, at about crotch height, and moving your legs back and forth.

The Hip Joint

Of particular importance to riders is the shape and characteristics of the iliofemoral (hip joint) ligament. In the normal standing position the iliofemoral ligament is twisted to the extreme. This twist prevents the thigh from bending back at the hip joint without tipping the pelvis forward and hollowing the back. Conversely, bending the hip joint forward, as to raise the knee, removes the twist and liberates the joint. Flexibility of the iliofemoral ligament to the point at which you can bend the hip joint backward without tipping the pelvis forward comes only after years of specific training. For the great majority of athletes, including equestrians, there is little backward flexibility of the hip joint. The

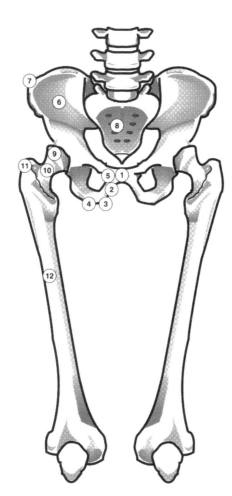

The pelvis and femur. (1) pubic crest; (2) descending pubic ramus; (3) ischial ramus; (4) ischial tuberosity; (5) ascending pubic ramus; (6) ilium; (7) iliac crest (hip bone); (8) sacrum; (9) head of femur (thigh bone); (10) neck; (11) greater trochanter; (12) body.

implications for riders are important: the normal sitting position, with the upper body resting on the ischial tuberosities, does not allow the knees to lower in place so that the rider's heels are under his or her center of gravity. Therefore, a tipping forward of the top part of the pelvis and a pulling up of the chest and chin, as if to sit tall, rocks the base of support forward from the ischial tuberosities onto the full length of the ischial ramus. This rocking forward of the pelvis allows a relaxation of the iliofemoral ligament and permits the thighs to fall straighter on each side of the horse. The result is a solid base of support further stabilized by long low legs, which enables the rider to better influence the maneuvers performed by the horse.

The Muscles of the Thigh

Many muscles form the human leg. I have limited our study to those that play an important role in effective horsemanship. I detail where each of these muscles attaches and the results of their contraction on the rider's legs and pelvis.

Looking at the back of the rider's leg we note the gluteus maximus. This large muscle begins at the crest of the ilium, the lower part of the sacrum, and the side of the coccyx. Its other extremity attaches to the femur. Located beneath the gluteus maximus and also tied to the ilium and the greater trochanter are the gluteus medius and the gluteus minimus. When contracted, the gluteus maximus and the gluteus medius extend, abduct, and rotate the thigh outward. The gluteus minimus rotates the thigh inward. Contraction of the gluteus maximus causes the seat to come out of the saddle and prevents forward and rearward rotation of the pelvis.

To experience this, sit on a hard bench and feel the hard surface of the bench with your seat bones. Hollow and round your back as you tip your pelvis forward and back. Now tighten the muscles of your seat and as you do so, feel yourself grow taller as your seat rises from the bench. Maintain the contraction in the muscles and try to tip your pelvis forward. You have just experienced what happens to the rider who

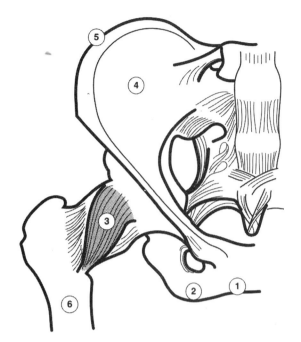

The twisted iliofemoral (hip joint) ligament. (1) ischial ramus; (2) ischial tuberosity; (3) iliofemoral ligament; (4) ilium; (5) iliac crest (hip bone); (6) femur.

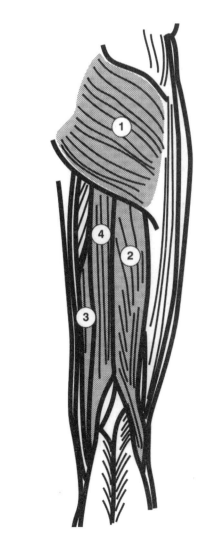

The muscles of the thigh, rear view. (1) gluteus maximus; (2) bicep femoris; (3) semitendinosus; (4) semimembranosus.

Muscles of the thigh, front view. (1) satorius; (2) adductors.

tightens the muscles of the seat: a loss of the deep seat and an inability to follow the movement of the horse's back because of a stiff midsection. Therefore, these "seat muscles" must only be used to spread the thighs and place them on each side of the saddle, after which they must remain totally inactive.

Still looking at a rear view of the rider's leg, we see the biceps femoris, the semitendinosus, and the semimembranosus. The semimembranosus and the semitendinosus originate from the ischial tuberosity, follow the inside of the thigh, and attach to the rear of the tibia (one of the two bones extending from the knee to the ankle). Both muscles act to rotate the lower leg inward. The biceps femoris also originates at the ischial tuberosity, comes down the back of the thigh, then curves to the outside of the tibia, where it ties. Contraction flexes the leg at the knee and rotates the lower leg outward without affecting the position of the thigh.

Because of their origin at the rear of the pelvis ring, these muscles serve to position the lower leg for various aids, tip the pelvis to the rear, and pull the seat bones down. When the knees are positioned low on the sides of the

horse, the alternate left leg/right leg downward pull of these muscles pulls each pelvic half alternately into the saddle. This process is essential to sitting in balance at the trot and is described in detail in chapter 8, which deals with seat aids.

Along with the description of these muscles and the detailing of their role, I must sound a serious warning. Strong and continuous contraction of these muscles causes immobility of the pelvis and results in a stiff midsection. The implications of this fact are serious: riders who make a marked muscular effort to keep their toes parallel to the horse's side, as prescribed by some riding schools, impede their ability to follow the horse's back and use their seat effectively.

At the front of the thigh is the satorius. A narrow but long muscle that originates at the front of the ilium and above the hip joint, the satorius crosses the front of the thigh and attaches on the inside of the tibia. It flexes the thigh on the pelvis, rotates the lower leg inward, and is helpful in tipping the pelvis forward when the rider's lower legs are low and stable.

Also seen from the front are the adductors. They extend from the pubic crest and ischial ramus to the inside of the femur. Riders often contract the adductors to stay in the saddle. However, contraction of the adductors completely immobilizes the pelvis and pushes the seat out of the saddle. To feel the effect of contracting the adductors, sit in your saddle and squeeze your thighs with as much force as you can. Feel your seat come out of the saddle? Now try to tip your pelvis forward or back while your maintain the squeeze. What you just experienced is an example of why one cannot ride effectively if he or she needs muscle strength to maintain balance: Contraction of many of the muscles in a rider's body are detrimental to moving with the horse. Yet effective riding cannot be accomplished without contraction of the correct muscles, in the proper measure and at the right time.

The Abdominal Muscles

Of the abdominal muscles, two are very important to effective horsemanship. They are the rectus abdominus and the obliques. The rectus abdominus extends from the crest of the pelvis to the cartilage of the fifth, sixth, and seventh ribs. The obliques run from the crest of the ilium to the lowest ribs. Through contraction of the rectus abdominus and the abdominal obliques the rider can draw the pubic crest closer to the ribcage, tip the pelvis rearward, and flatten the back. As further explained in chapter 8, this contraction of the abdominal muscles is essential to driving the horse forward at a walk and lope.

The Back Muscles

Powerful muscles run on each side of the spine from the rear of the pelvis all the way to the top of the spine. So far as concerns the rider, contraction of the back muscles tips the pelvis forward and stabilizes the spine.

With the anatomical basics behind us, we are prepared to discuss the all-important independent seat.

THE INDEPENDENT SEAT

Essential to effective horsemanship, the independent seat is characterized by stability of the upper body, suppleness of the midsection, adherence of the thighs, fixity of the legs, and ease of movements in the shoulders, neck, and arms. These characteristics lead to an ability to apply any aid or combination of aids without forcing a loss of balance or unwanted application of nondesirable cues; your body is completely steady and you are able to counterbalance any possible jolt or jerk that might upset your seat's continuous contact with the horse's back.

Every one of these characteristics is important, and all are interrelated. A rider cannot display stability of the upper body without having an equal measure of suppleness in the midsection. And adherence of the thighs to the saddle is necessary if the upper body is to remain stable and the shoulders and arms are to move with ease. Let's look at each of the characteristics of the independent seat.

Fixity of the rider's legs refers to legs that are always under complete control of the rider. Never do the fixed legs move, apply pressure, or release pressure, consequently cuing the horse, without the carefully reasoned thought of the rider. The fixed legs that do not happen to bump the horse at the wrong time through the course of a fast or complicated maneuver take longer to achieve. Their development parallels that of the other characteristics of the independent seat and comes after many hours of riding, exercising, and strong focusing.

Because they are so closely attached to the rider's base of support—the seat bones—the thighs can play an important role in maintaining an independent seat. Thighs that adhere to the saddle widen the rider's base of support. The thighs adhere to the saddle when the inside flat part of the thigh is placed against the saddle. Thighs are a barrier to an independent seat when the rider uses the adductors to squeeze the saddle, thereby causing stiffness in the midsection, or when they are so open that the round muscular rear of the thighs rests against the saddle. In the latter instance, instead of serving as stabilizers, the thighs roll back and forth on those long narrow muscles, causing unsteady and haphazard lower-leg aids.

Suppleness of the midsection is a prerequisite to continuous seat contact, steady balance, and controlled aids. Suppleness does not mean total relaxation of all the muscles but rather flexibility of the body through refined control of the muscles. Since a stiff midsection and hip joints cannot absorb the jolts of the horse's back, the body bounces up and down, never landing at the same place in the saddle. The stiffer the midsection, the less it is able to absorb the shocks. The more the rider bounces, the more his or her center of gravity is out of sync with that of the horse. Naturally, the more the rider finds him- or herself out of balance, the more he or she stiffens, grips with the legs, and pulls on the reins to keep astride. A rider searching for balance this way sends all sorts of mixed cues to the horse and cannot refine the application of his or her aids. Stability of the upper body and ease of movements in the shoulders, neck, and arms are also achieved through balance. Balance, then, is a foundational element of the independent seat and effective horsemanship.

Riding in Balance

Balance is the state of equilibrium through which a body's mass is equally distributed above its base of support. For instance, the circus's tightrope walker can complete his precarious stunt only when there is an equal amount of his weight on each side of the narrow rope. More weight to the left of the rope and he falls into the net. Comparatively, the rider's base of support is his or her seat bones. To be in balance, a rider must have the same amount of body mass to the front, rear, left, and right of his or her base. In horsemanship, balance is further complicated by the horse's constantly moving center of gravity; the tightrope moves. To be in balance with the horse, the rider's center of gravity must remain directly above the horse's center of gravity while he performs intricate maneuvers at different speeds.

Balance is the only way to be secure on horseback. Any muscular effort made to stay on the horse causes rigidity and makes it impossible for the rider to feel the horse and give the proper aids. Muscular effort also causes soreness in muscles not normally used by the human body. In addition to your own soreness, your muscular struggle leads to soreness in your horse. As your center of gravity moves to the left, right, back, and front of his, he moves to place himself underneath it to more easily carry you in balance. Therefore, resist the temptation to remain in balance by squeezing the thighs or hanging onto the reins. Such stiffening of the joints causes your base of support to bounce off the horse's back to a degree more or less dependent on the gait travelled and the activity performed. This stiffness—which is all too often present in very subtle yet harmful doses in experienced riders—results in hard, heavy, and uncoordinated actions on the part of the rider. For this reason, a stiff and unyielding rider cannot bring a well-schooled horse to perform properly.

Standing in balance with both feet on the barn floor is quite simple. The problem a rider faces is that the moving horse must constantly shift his center of gravity and, to remain a balanced team, the rider must make continuous adjustments. Watch the cutting horse as he stops hard from a 15-mile-per-hour run, turns over his hocks 180 degrees, stops again, then turns 90 degrees to face the cow, all in a matter of two seconds or less. All through those moves, the horse's center of gravity shifts considerably several times and the rider has to adjust his or her center of gravity to stay with the horse and even help him control the cow. A rider unable to adjust his or her center of gravity would have lost balance and found him or herself leaning over the horse's neck or even sitting on the ground beside him.

Every riding performance depends on balance. From the equitation rider to the barrel racer, cutter, or reiner, balance is essential to harmony and feel.

Developing Balance

Balance is developed through feel. It is not an attribute you can develop through deductive reasoning. Just as the six-month-old baby feels her way to sitting up by herself and later feels her way to taking those first steps without falling, so it is with developing riding balance. The parents do not outline to the child "the six steps to walking without falling." The child's ability to walk eventually comes from sensory responses of his or her nervous system that control, in a way no one can teach, the muscles needed to walk without falling. Balance is instinctive. Hence, by going in and out of balance, the rider's nervous system learns to control his or her muscular reactions so that the rider's center of gravity can stay in harmony with that of the horse.

As a rider you have at your disposal several ways to develop balance. All have their part to play in the process and therefore are essential to achieving an independent seat. Riding a number of different horses, in an arena and in open country, affords you the opportunity to feel different rhythms and experience different reactions. Riding over cavaletti, or crossing natural obstacles such as creeks, fallen trees, ditches, and steep hills develops your feel for the horse's center of balance. Riding with your eyes closed forces you to maintain balance by feel rather than by visually locating your horse and seeing what his next move will be. Also beneficial to the development of confidence and balance are a number of exercises performed on horseback, including riding without stirrups.

Riding without Stirrups

Initially, stirrups are necessary to afford you some degree of security and comfort. Until you become accomplished in the art, however, riding with stirrups often causes you to adopt a faulty and ineffective position: your knees rise and open up, your seat rests behind the horse's center of gravity and behind the motion, and your upper body leans forward ahead of the driving aids. On the other hand, when you ride without stirrups your seat sinks to the bottom of the saddle. Your hip and knee joints relax and open up as your legs become long, low, and heavy. As a result, your center of gravity slides forward and low as more of your body touches the saddle and you get a feeling of fullness in your seat.

Please be advised, however, that although riding without stirrups is a very efficient way of developing an independent seat, it must be practiced with caution. Exaggerated or ill-advised usage may result in a tear in the groin muscles and an actual regression in the improvement of your riding. Short periods at low paces such as jog, walk, and lope, while at the same time maintaining suppleness and easiness, are key to long-lasting benefits.

EXERCISES ON HORSEBACK

Exercises on horseback can eliminate undesirable muscle stiffness, correct faults in body position, and help the nervous system develop a feel for balance. When a beginning rider focuses on the correct execution of the exercises, he or she grows less afraid of falling and confidence gradually replaces paralyzing apprehensions.

Armed with determination, someone who has never been on horseback can develop balance in a matter of months by doing these drills under the eye of an experienced coach. Even experienced riders have much to gain from these exercises.

To fully benefit from them, a rider should not have to worry about where his or her horse is going. Therefore, it is best to use a quiet horse, on a lunge line. All riders should wear protective headgear when working on the exercises. All the drills should be done at the walk first, then at the trot, and finally at the lope.

Arm Exercises

The main purpose of these exercises is to relax and supple the shoulder muscles and ensure independence of the arms from the movements made by the rest of the body. Single-arm exercises also aim at developing an independence of each arm from the other.

Hold your arms stretched above your head while you keep your head high and look up. Concentrate on the feel of the movements of the horse through your seat and the vibrations the horse imparts to your body. Relax every joint in your body, from your ankles to the tips of your fingers.

Begin with the right arm, stretching it out and rotating it up and back toward the horse's tail. Keep the arm fully extended. Watch your hand as it goes around to the back, low beside your hip, in front of you, then up again. Always rotate from front to back. Do ten repetitions with each arm. This exercise helps you sit upright on the horse and relax your shoulders.

Rotate your arms alternately, i.e. as the right arm rises, the left arm lowers. A variation of this exercise is to bend one arm as you rotate the other. Again, these exercises aim at relaxing the shoulder muscles and developing independent aids.

Midsection Exercises

The purpose of these exercises is to relax, supple, and strengthen the back, lumbar, and abdominal muscles and to facilitate the movement of the lumbar vertebrae.

With your feet out the stirrups, lean forward and touch the right stirrup leather with your left hand, and vice versa. Focus on keeping your seat in the saddle and your lower leg from sliding back in the horse's flank. In addition to building a seat, this drill is very beneficial in developing an independent lower leg. This exercise is helpful if you ride with a hollow or stiff lower back, but avoid this exercise if you ride with a round back.

With your feet out of the stirrups, rotate and touch the right stifle of the horse with your left hand, and vice versa. Turn your head and watch your hand as you push it down the side of the horse. Go as low as you can without allowing your knees to come up. This exercise is very beneficial to riders who are stiff in the upper body.

Hold your arms straight out to the side and rotate your upper body and head, first to the left and then to the right. Focus on rotating in the lower back, making sure that your left knee does not rise as you turn to the right, and vice versa. This is an opportunity to develop a seat that is independent from your upper body movements.

Leg Exercises

The following leg exercises aim at developing a long, supple, strong leg. When properly executed over a period of time, the exercises serve to relax the hip, knee, and ankle joints, enabling the rider to move one leg without affecting any movement in the other leg or other parts of the body. Again, this is the essence of the independent seat and is paramount to upper-level equitation and horse training.

While holding your arms out and to the side, elevate your right knee so that your ankle is about the same height as the horse's withers. Keep your right foot away from the horse or saddle and your left foot out of the stirrup. Count to five and then let your leg down. Alternate between your left and right leg. This exercise is excellent for developing balance, particularly when performed at the trot and lope. A variation of this exercise is to lift both knees up at the same time. In this position your sensory system is truly challenged as your horse trots and lopes circles. The ability to perform this exercise guarantees that you do not need your legs and stirrups to remain in balance and are well on your way to achieving an independent seat.

Still riding without stirrups, flex your right knee slowly and bring your foot up to the saddle. Focus on not moving the other leg, the upper body, or the right thigh as you bring the ankle up to your hand. Grab your ankle with your right hand and pull the leg up and back as far as you can. Hold for five seconds and release. Alternate the left and right leg. In addition to correcting a leg carried too far forward, this exercise develops the independence of the legs from each other as well as the independence of each leg from the upper body. Again, a skill essential in all aspects of horsemanship.

Always with your feet out of the stirrups, kick both feet away from the horse at the same time. Be sure the motion of the legs is at a right angle to the horse and not toward the front. This exercise stretches and relaxes the hip joint and adductors and lets your seat settle deep into the saddle while your leg gets long and heavy. To prevent injuring your groin, be careful not to kick too hard at the beginning.

Execute with each foot, through a slow and regular movement, a circle from top to bottom and from the outside to the inside without moving the leg. This exercise supples and strengthens the ankle joints and builds independence of the aids.

Effectiveness

To be effective, these exercises must be executed correctly, completely, and repeated often. Each exercise is particularly adapted to correcting a specific problem or developing independence of the aids in a specific part of the body. For instance, someone who rides with a hollow back is encouraged to execute exercises which round and stretch the lower back muscles: lifting the knees and leaning forward to touch the stirrups. A stiff-backed rider needs to practice all of the exercises that involve bending the back. A rider with stiff, closed shoulders needs to spend much time on the arm rotation exercises while he or she looks high and far. One whose lower leg is too far forward will benefit from pulling on his or her ankle to bring the knee down and back and place the pelvis correctly.

A basic test of your success at attaining your goal of an independent seat is your ability to sit in balance without reins and stirrups at all three gaits. The ultimate test of your success at attaining an independent seat is the ability to school several horses to the highest performance level in various events.

PHYSICAL CONDITIONING

As you understand by now, proper and effective horsemanship is based in part on attaining three important characteristics: flexibility of all joints; strength of specific muscles, such as the abdominal and back muscles; and complete cognitive and instinctive control of the muscles responsible for each body part used in riding. Aerobic fitness, as you will see, is also important to horsemanship. This essential fitness, flexibility, and strength can be developed through selected exercises. These exercises can be performed on the floor of your home or tack room, the lobby area of your riding club, or the alleyway of your barn. Unless indicated otherwise, repeat each set of the following stetches and exercises five times for maximum benefit.

Flexibility

Stretching exercises are an effective way to improve the range of motion in the rider's joints. For these exercises to be beneficial, however, you must warm up your muscles before stretching them. Active walking is a suitable way to warm the muscles. Once the muscles are warm, they can be stretched progressively. Stretch the particular joint, but only to a point at which you feel mild tension. Maintain the position for approximately twenty seconds. Repeat the stretch two or three times.

No pain or discomfort should be associated with the stretching exercises. If pain or discomfort occurs while you hold the position, you are probably stretching too far. In such instances, slowly ease into a more comfortable position. Pain is indicative of microscopic tears in the muscles. These tears lead to the formation of scar tissue, which in turn interferes with blood flow and reduces elasticity.

Flexibility of the hip joint is key to proper positioning of the thigh and absorption of the shocks generated by the horse's back. Therefore, exercises designed to stretch the iliofemoral ligament and the strong muscles of the thigh should be part of your routine.

With your legs wide apart, your feet pointing straight ahead, and your hands on your hips, shift your weight over one leg and stretch the adductors of the thighs. Keep your knee above your foot, your other leg straight, and both feet flat on the ground. Hold for twenty seconds, then repeat with the other leg.

This exercise stretches the muscles of the lower leg. Facing a wall, in this case a trailer, place one foot in front of the other. Lean forward over the front leg and flex it while you keep your back leg straight. Hold for twenty seconds. Repeat.

This exercise also stretches the muscles of the lower leg, making it possible to hold the heels lower than the toes. Keep your back straight, your head up, your feet flat on the ground as you lower your body by bending your knees. Hold for twenty seconds. Repeat.

With your back leg stretched behind you and your toes pointed to the ground, lower your weight and stretch the iliofemoral ligament by bending your front leg. Be careful not to hollow your back since doing so will result in a tipping of the pelvis and prevent stretching in the hip joint. Also be sure the knee of the front leg remains centered over the foot to prevent injury to the hip joint ligament. Hold for twenty seconds. Alternate.

Strength of the Midsection

Strength of some muscle groups is essential to effective horsemanship. And nowhere is this more important than in the muscles of the midsection. Well-toned, hard abdominal and back muscles are more responsive than soft ones to the commands of the nervous system. Their response is more accurate and longer lasting than that of muscles with less tone. This is important to the rider who rides one hour a day, and even more so to the rider who rides several hours a day. Since strong muscles are essential to maintaining proper posture, several hours of riding leave the muscles that support the upper body fatigued. Poor posture develops and little by little becomes a bad habit. Effectiveness is soon lost and riding injuries such as a sore back or pulled groin muscles cause further fatigue and faulty positioning. Four of the suggested exercises aim at strengthening the abdominal and back muscles.

This exercise strengthens the upper abdominals. Lie on the carpet with knees bent and feet flat. Hold your hands beside your head and keep your elbows back to prevent pulling on your neck. Lift your upper torso until your shoulder blades are off the carpet. A thirty-degree angle with the carpet is sufficient for maximum results. Hold for three seconds, then lower your upper torso. Repeat until abdominal muscles are fatigued.

This exercise strengthens the abdominal obliques. Lie on your back with knees bent and thighs perpendicular to the carpet. Again place your hands on each side of your head. Keeping your elbows back and your thighs upright, lift both shoulders simultaneously off the carpet, then twist to one side, pointing your elbow to your opposite knee. Hold for three seconds. Repeat until fatigued.

This is one of the best exercises for strengthening the erector spinea (those muscles that play the biggest role in keeping the vertebrae and spinal disk together and in place). Lie face down on a table and have someone hold your legs, with your hips level with the edge of the table. Place your hands behind your head and lower your torso until you feel your back muscles stretch. From this position round your back as much as possible and then raise your torso until it is parallel with the ground. Lower your torso and repeat. Be careful not to raise your torso so high that your back actually hollows. Such hyperextension places a tremendous amount of stress on the vertebrae and does very little for the muscles.

This exercise also stretches the abdominal obliques. Stand with your feet approximately twenty inches apart. Hold one arm above your head while you reach down your leg as far as possible with the other arm. Hold for twenty seconds. Slowly return to erect position. Do not bounce. Alternate.

Weight Control and Aerobic Fitness

A rider's weight can have serious consequences on his or her effectiveness. Extra body fat lodges around internal organs and under the skin, disrupting normal body functions. Aside from the physiological harm, body fat actually hinders the rider by forcing his or her seat bones and legs farther away from the horse. The larger legs and buttocks tend to roll back and forth as the horse moves, diminishing the steadiness of the aids. This inherent instability combined with the greater upper body weight make it difficult for the rider to find balance. Several good books are available on diet and weight control and you may want to consult a dietitian on the subject.

Another important way to increase your fitness level is aerobic exercise. While most effective in controlling weight and generally improving quality of life, the benefits of aerobic exercise to the rider's mind are most attractive. In his book *The Aerobics Way*, Dr. Kenneth H. Cooper refers to studies that show improvement in "emotional stability, imagination, self-assurance, and self-sufficiency" (page 176). Dr. Cooper and other researchers credit these mental benefits of aerobic exercise to the fit body's improved ability to carry oxygen and glucose to the brain. Dr. Cooper reports of one other study which shows that "aerobic fitness results in improvement in the following seven categories of the thinking process: originality of thought; duration of concentration; mental response time; ability to change topics and subjects quickly; depth of thinking; duality of thoughts—the ability to entertain a number of ideas at once; and finally, mental tenacity." As outlined in the previous chapter, every one of these mental abilities is fundamental to effective horsemanship, horse training, and horse showing. Therefore a rider's exercise program should include aerobics.

Walking is a simple exercise, yet one of the most beneficial aerobic exercises one can ever engage in. Done correctly, walking improves cardiovascular capacity and strengthens the arms, legs, lower back, and stomach muscles. A brisk walk necessitates a significant rotation of the pelvis, which requires effort from the abdominal muscles. The result is a flatter stomach and a stronger, more supple midsection.

Aerobic exercise is too large a topic to discuss at length in this book. I recommend riders read Dr. Cooper's book or some other reputable work and follow the instructions for aerobic conditioning.

The exercises suggested in this section have been selected to enhance the riding athlete's flexibility, strength, general fitness, and ultimately his or her effectiveness on horseback. They should be performed four to five times a week to improve conditioning. Consult a physician before beginning and be sure you remain well within your comfort zone for the first few weeks.

CHAPTER 5

Body Position

Crookedness in the rider has serious consequences on the horse's performance.

The rider's body position is often as specialized as the performance horse himself. Maneuvers required of the cutting horse are much different from those expected of the pleasure horse. And there is little apparent resemblance between a winning barrel run and a world champion reining horse run. Nevertheless, to be functionally correct, the position of the rider must not hinder the horse and must enable him or her to apply the aids in a quiet but effective way, at the right time, at the right place on the horse, and with the right intensity.

Good body position is important in all types of riding, for bad posture in the saddle can potentially lead to injury to both rider and horse. Many horses exhibit various difficulties in performing certain exercises simply because their riders sit crooked and pull the horse out of balance. This imbalance leads the horse to compensate by tightening certain muscles and adopting positions that may eventually lead to unsoundness. Even in its most quiet forms of riding, the horse's center of gravity shifts constantly and the rider's body position must be such as to permit these natural movements to occur unobstructed. Riders who unconsciously place more weight in one stirrup than the other, or ride with one shoulder ahead of the other, or lean to one side, or exhibit a host of other faulty positions, hinder their horses' balance and create barriers for themselves. For these reasons, it is important for every rider to master this basic position if he or she is to succeed at the more demanding specialized events.

This basic equitation seat is suitable for all slow work on the flat. This is the seat used to apply most of the training on the performance horse regardless of his vocation and is also the seat upon which all other specialized positions are based. When in the correct position, the rider is better able to feel the responses of the horse—a key to correct application of the aids and effective horsemanship.

Before I describe the position, I need to make the point that just as this chapter on body position was preceded by the one on independent seat, so should a rider develop suppleness and relaxation of the joints before trying to maintain a specific position. A rider who tries to adopt a steady alignment of the body before developing suppleness and relaxation may never lose his or her initial stiffness. For the purpose of describing the position, I will begin at the head, talk my way down the rider's body, and finish with the hands.

To describe the overall position: a vertical line leaving the ground at a ninety-degree angle should touch the back of your heel, pass

An imaginary line perpendicular to the ground should touch your heel and pass through your hip, shoulder, and ear.

through your hip, your shoulder, and your ear. This position places your center of gravity, which is located just ahead of your spine and below your rib cage, above your seat bones and lets your legs fall correctly positioned for proper application of leg aids.

Hold your head up and your neck long. Your head represents twelve to fourteen percent of your body weight and any fault in its position will definitely cause imbalances in the upper body. Looking at the ground or at your horse lowers your chin and causes your back and shoulders to fall forward, putting your body out of balance. Your chest caves in and your midsection and legs become ineffective in driving the horse forward or laterally. If you must look at the ground, keep your head up and lower your eyes rather than your chin.

Sit tall in the saddle, stretching your upper body upward as if you were trying to relieve the nagging pain caused by someone constantly pulling up on the hair at the top of your head. Sitting tall is a preventative measure for a number of position faults, not the least of which are a round back, a hanging head, and a collapsed waist. Sitting tall also pulls up your rib cage and enables you to use your abdominal muscles much more effectively according to the ways described in chapter 8.

Seen from the rear, your shoulders should be square. They should be held in line with your hips, with a feeling that your shoulder blades are touching each other in the back. Be careful not to twist your upper body and carry one shoulder ahead of the other when riding with one hand. A shoulder held higher than the other, or one carried ahead of the other, shows that you place more weight on this particular seat bone. This always results in your horse stepping short on that side and eventually having difficulty turning or changing leads in that direction. Be sure to keep your shoulders relaxed. They are an important link between your body and the horse's mouth, and because of all the muscles that attach them to your rib cage, any stiffness in the shoulders is sure to affect the entire performance. To help relax your shoulder muscles, imagine them as jelly and let them vibrate in rhythm with the movements of the horse.

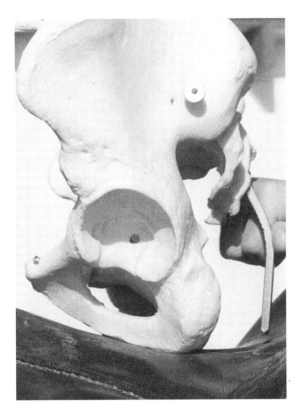

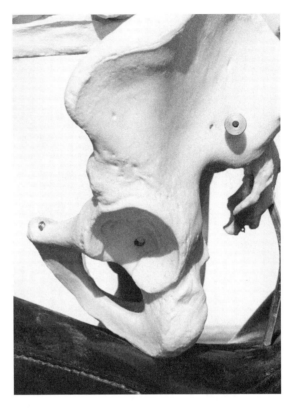

The pelvis of a rider who sits correctly would be in the same position as this cast. The rider's center of gravity is directly above her seat bones (her base of support). The forward tilt of her pelvis allows her leg to fall lower on the horse, thereby increasing its efficiency. Note that she sits on the full length of her ischial ramus, not only on the ischial tuberosities.

This is the position of the pelvis in a rider who sits on her hip pockets. The hip bone tilts back and the back is actually round. The spine and center of gravity are not directly above the base of support, in this case the ischial tuberosities only, but rather behind it. Because of the twisted shape of the hip joint ligament, as described in the previous chapter, this position makes it difficult to correctly place the thigh and lower leg on the horse. This is the position to adopt when your horse approaches a barrel or stops hard in front of a cow. However, since it results in a high knee and an ineffective lower leg and midsection, resume the straight back as soon as possible to regain effectiveness with your leg and seat aids.

The position of your back depends largely on the way you sit in the saddle. Riders who sit on their "hip pockets" rather than on the full length of their seat bones show a round back. Their hipbones fall behind the vertical line described earlier. Others sit on the front part of their seat bones and their hipbones fall ahead of the vertical line. Their back is hollow. Both of these positions are ineffective in sitting in rhythm with the horse at any gait and are even more inefficient when it comes to driving or holding the horse with your seat. Your back should be flat, with no curvature to the right or to the left. The muscles of your back must continually exercise strength and flexibility in order to keep the back straight but supple enough to absorb the movements of the horse's back.

Your seat bones are your base of support, and your hips are an indication of how balanced that base actually is. For maximum suppleness and effectiveness in the saddle, keep your hipbones (iliac crest: the bones you feel when you place your hands on your hips) directly above your seat bones. This position places your base of support directly below your center of gravity and facilitates riding in balance. Your buttocks should rest in the bottom of the saddle rather than against the cantle. Seen from the rear, your hips should be level, with your tailbone directly above the horse's spine.

One of the most common and most restrictive faults you can possibly exhibit is the collapsed

From the rear, the imaginary line should run straight down your spine through the middle of the cantle, through the horse's spine, and on down the middle of his body.

This rider suffers from what is referred to as the "turkey head syndrome." Because her head is not in equilibrium above the base of support, her neck and upper back muscles are tense from holding her head from falling forward even more. This stiffness in the upper body is inevitably communicated to the horse's mouth, where the evident abruptness results in bracing and poor performance.

This rider braces against the cantle and leans forward in a failed attempt to remain balanced. The bracing and stiffness in her legs and midsection render her completely ineffective in controlling her horse's body for any exercise, from transitions to correct turns.

hip. The collapsed hip is very recognizable from the rear: the rider sits to one side of the horse and leans in the other direction in order to maintain balance. The side to which the rider sits carries more weight than the other, the shoulder is higher and the leg feels longer. By contrast, on the less weighted side of the rider, the leg feels shorter and the toes often point down in order to reach the stirrup. The shoulder is lower since the rider leans in that direction to counterbalance the weighted side of his or her body. The result is ineffective leg aid from the lighter side and a horse that tends to fall in the direction of the weighted seat bone. In other words, the horse readily moves his hindquarters in the direction of the light side but his shoulders move quite freely in the direction of the heavy side. This crookedness in the rider has very serious consequences on the horse's performance. Have you ever wondered why your barrel horse runs wide at the first barrel and falls into the second one? Or why your cutting horse is always two-tracking and short on one side while working the cow parallel and long on the other? The answer may rest in part in your collapsed hip, which causes you to unconsciously apply uneven aids and develop your horse unevenly.

Once entrenched, the collapsed hip is very difficult to correct. For if you have been sitting crooked all along, you will feel crooked even when you are sitting straight. Your coach can help you recognize your collapsed hip, but you must take it upon yourself to overcome the fault. A most effective way is to feel for equal weight on each stirrup at all times. Also helpful in balancing your seat in the middle of the horse are all the exercises described in chapter 4, performed while lungeing on the circle, particularly those involving lifting the legs above the swells alternately and one at a time.

Your hip joints should be relaxed to allow for a wide angle between your hips and thighs. The wider the angle, the lower your knee, and the lower your lower leg on the side of the horse. A narrow angle leads to a high knee, a chair seat, and an ineffective lower leg and seat. A long and low leg allows for more control of the horse's body through more effective leg aids. To help

This rider exhibits what is called the "fetus syndrome." This faulty position, most often seen in beginners but also to a certain degree in more experienced riders, is characterized by a tense upper body, collapsed waist, and high knees. All effectiveness is essentially lost due to the high center of gravity and typical nervousness. This fault is best corrected by exercises on the lunge line, using a quiet horse.

Your foot should fall naturally on the side of the horse, slightly pointed to the outside.

Holding the foot parallel to the horse's side causes the knee to turn toward and grip the saddle. The muscular effort necessary to maintain this position leads to a tightening of the entire leg and thigh muscles and drives the seat out of the saddle.

Excessively turned out toes cause the knee to point away from the saddle, resulting in a loss of stability in the thighs and lower leg.

This rider demonstrates the most difficult fault to correct: the collapsed hip. Her seat bones have shifted to the left of the center of the horse. Her right hip has collapsed, her right shoulder has gone down, and her right stirrup feels too long. In this collapsed hip position, she does not have effective control of her aids and will eventually develop crookedness in her horse.

relax your hip joint, imagine your leg is so heavy that it could pull your hip joint out of the socket.

Your thighs should fall loosely against the saddle. Tight thighs lead to tight knees and stiff lower legs held away from the horse's sides. If your thighs are round and of the fleshy type, use your hand and move the flabby flesh to the back of your leg once you are in the saddle. Sitting on your fleshy thighs results in an unstable base of support and lower leg. Your knee should be relaxed, opening or closing according to the aid applied.

The stirrups should be adjusted so that there is a bend in the rider's knee, bringing the heel in line with the hip, shoulder, and ear. Check the stirrup length and the position of your lower leg by standing up in the saddle. If you can place your hands between your seat and the saddle when standing, your stirrups are at the correct length. If you lose your balance to the front as you stand, your lower leg is too far behind the cinch. If you lose your balance to the rear, the

opposite is true, and your lower leg is too far forward. This position of your lower leg is most effective when it comes to aiding the horse into various maneuvers. Your lower legs should be in contact with the horse at all times, not applying pressure but feeling the horse's sides and following their movements. Holding the lower legs away from the horse means stiffness in the legs and aids that are not ready to act invisibly at the precise moment required for smooth performance.

The position of your foot should be the same as it is when you are walking, with the toes turned slightly away from the horse. This position allows for full leg contact with the horse's side all the way down to the ankle and facilitates bending application of the leg aids through the use of the proper thigh muscles. Avoid trying to keep your foot parallel to the horse's side. This forced position drives your knee into the saddle and forces your lower leg away from the horse's side. In addition, holding your feet parallel to the horse's sides renders your bicep femoris (thigh muscle active in bending the leg at the knee) ineffective when you need to squeeze both legs on the horse. In this case, the only muscles to use would be the adductors of the thighs. We saw in chapter 4 the detrimental results of tightening your adductors: immobility of your seat and hip joint, tension throughout your body, and inability to aid the horse.

Wear the stirrups on the balls of your feet, with your heels lower than your toes. Just like all your other joints, your ankle must remain flexible to fulfill its role of shock absorber.

Your elbows should fall naturally at your sides. No effort should be made to hold them close to the body, neither should they be held wide as the wings of a bird flying off a fence post.

Your hands should be relaxed. A stiff hand causes your wrist and forearm to stiffen. Tight muscles in the hand reduce its sensitivity and lend the rein effect much unwanted roughness. Tensing the forearm muscles also results in rigidity in the arm and shoulder. The height at which you carry your hands depends on the purpose of the riding and the responses from the horse. Generally, carry your hands just above and slightly ahead of the swells. When riding with one hand, extend your forearm toward the horse's head. Hold your rein hand at the same height as the horn and slightly ahead of it. Your free hand can be carried in two ways: your arm relaxed

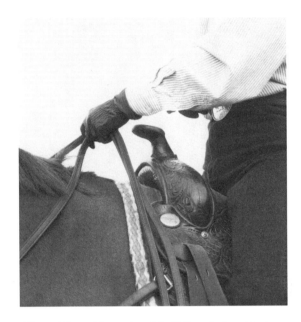

When riding with one hand, hold the rein hand just above and slightly ahead of the horn. Hold the free hand at about the same height as the rein hand and slightly behind the swells.

and hanging naturally at your side, or your arm flexed at the elbow and your hand close to the swells. Keep your hand relaxed and your fingers slightly closed.

Correct body position is more than just looking good on the horse. In fact, it has very little to do with looking good on the horse but everything to do with riding in balance and rhythm with every move your horse makes. Sometimes, this balance can be kept only by altering the basic position slightly, in such events as reining, cutting, barrel racing, etc. Nevertheless, you cannot slightly alter the basic position unless you have mastered it. Never stop focusing on your position. Your effectiveness depends on it.

CHAPTER 6

Posting

Posting tests your independent seat.

Posting is the action of rising from the horse's back as he trots. It was discovered in England in the eighteenth century by a postillion, hence the name *posting*. It was immediately adopted as a way of softening the bone-jarring blow of sitting the trot during extended riding periods. Posting is often used on rides when loping is not practical or would be too exhausting for the horse, and covering a long distance in a relatively short time makes long trotting the horse a reasonable gait to travel. An example of this may be trail riders or cowboys moving cattle.

In this chapter I will talk about the body position most effective while posting, but first I will uncover the dynamics of posting.

THE DYNAMICS

As he trots, your horse pushes himself forward and up with each diagonal pair of legs. Between each push is a moment of suspension during which the horse's back reaches the apex of the flight. The upward motion the horse needs to move himself forward sends you up above his back. Since you are lighter than your horse you will be in the air for a longer period of time and the apex of your flight will be higher than that of your horse. Therefore, you will begin your descent later than your horse. By the time you are halfway through your descent toward your saddle, your horse has already touched the ground and is again on the ascent. This collision between your curve and your horse's curve of travel is what makes sitting the long trot a demanding,

71

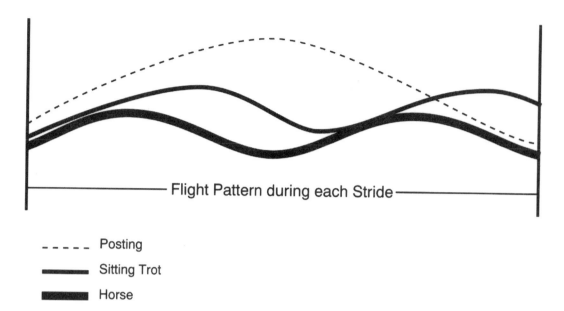

— Flight Pattern during each Stride —

- - - - -   Posting

▬▬▬▬   Sitting Trot

▬▬▬▬   Horse

This diagram illustrates the flight patterns of your body and of your horse's body during one trotting stride. Since you are lighter than your horse, your apex is higher and you remain in the air longer. Therefore, at the sitting trot your horse has time to touch the ground and push himself up again before you reach the bottom of your flight. Meeting your horse on his way up while your are descending is the source of the jarring you may feel at the sitting trot. Note the common descent you and your horse engage when you post. Rising at the beginning of the stride and sitting at its completion lets you descend in unison with your horse and makes it more comfortable to ride a ground-covering trot.

if not rough, challenge to beginner and even intermediate riders.

When you post, you avoid the collision of your descending seat with the ascending saddle by allowing yourself to go up higher than you would at the sitting trot. In going higher you remain in the air for a longer period of time than you would if you were sitting. This longer flight time lets your horse land and push off with the other diagonal pair of legs, reach the apex of his second flight and begin his descent, at which point you join with the saddle again and both of you complete the descent. The horse pushes off again and the cycle is repeated for another stride.

Obviously, the diagonal pair of legs to which you rise and sit work harder, to push you up and receive you on the descent, than the other diagonal pair. To even out the amount of effort required of each diagonal pair and to develop the horse equally, change diagonals on a regular basis. Changing diagonals is simply done by sitting two pushoffs in a row rather than rising. For instance, if you were to count "up, down, up, down" as you rise and sit, you would

count "up, down, up, down, up, down, down, up, down, up" and so on as you post. The two continuous down times lets the horse push you off with the other diagonal.

Changing diagonals every time you change direction is a good way to ensure an even workload for each pair of legs. When turning either left or right, correct posting calls for you to sit as the inside hind leg/outside front leg land and rise as they push up and forward. This sitting and rising on the inside hind leg drives the leg deeper under the horse's body and favors a more forward gait.

POSITION

Balance is key to correct posting just as in all other riding situations. As you recall from chapter 4, balance is reached when your center of gravity is positioned equally above your base of support. In posting, your base of support moves forward from your seat bones to the balls of your feet in the stirrups. Hence, to balance

This rider leans forward slightly at the sitting stage of posting, moving his center of balance from his seat bones to the balls of his feet. This change in position makes it easier for the horse to push him up and ensures he does not land heavily on the horse's back. (Photo: Ted Gard)

At the top of the rise, the angles at the back of his knee and the front of his hip have opened. His seat has moved forward and above the balls of his feet. His upper body is straight, as if he were pulled ahead and up by his belt buckle. (Photo: Ted Gard)

yourself over this new base of support while in the sitting stage of the trot, move your center of gravity slightly ahead of its normal position at the walk. To effect this change, lean forward very slightly as you sit down in the saddle. This position moves your center of gravity from where it normally is, immediately in front of your spine and just below your rib-cage, to a new location closer to the front of your body. This more frontal center of gravity lets *you go* up higher and stay up longer than you would otherwise. I must emphasize the words *very slightly*. To lean forward would place your center of gravity much ahead of your horse's, and make it difficult for you to ride him forward and apply your aids effectively. For this same reason, do not maintain the forward lean as you rise, but rather bring your pelvis forward and under your shoulders as you reach the apex of your rise. In

other words, your shoulders remain in the same position but your seat moves forward and back underneath them as you rise and descend.

Important to your ability to ride the posting trot in rhythm is the position of your legs in relation to your upper body. Just as with the normal sitting position, your legs should be placed so that your heels are directly under your seat bones. If you typically ride with your lower legs too far forward and your seat braced against the cantle, it will be impossible for your horse to send you up in rhythm. In this position your weight is behind your horse's center of gravity and behind your base of support. This makes it very difficult for you to attain the apex of your flight and you will land heavily against the back of the saddle, jarring your horse's back and possibly making him sore. Also, you will find yourself falling back into the saddle twice for each of the horse's diagonal pushes. Your legs should remain directly under your body when you ascend and descend, just as they should be when you ride your horse at the walk.

As with all other gaits, your joints must be flexible, as their opening and closing is essential to maintaining balance. Obviously, your knee and hip joint must open and close, but so should your elbow joint. Failure to open and close the elbow as you post causes your hand to go up and down and sends hard, painful messages to your horse's mouth. Feel your knee, hip, and elbow joints open and close as you rise and sit. Be sure to keep your head high and straight. Hanging the head, rounding the shoulders, collapsing at the waist or hip, all have the same negative effects during posting as they do when you are sitting.

You should have the same amount of weight in your stirrups, whether you are ascending or descending. If you feel more weight in your stirrups while ascending, you are pushing yourself up rather than letting your horse do it. Let your horse push you up instead of lifting yourself by force. There is an important difference: it is almost impossible to be in rhythm with your horse's back if you are pushing yourself up. This means you do not land softly in the saddle as your horse begins his descent and you most likely are bumping your horse's back to a point of soreness or, at the very least, stiffness and bracing. Too much distance between your seat and the saddle is another indication that you are lifting yourself. Never should there be more than one inch between the saddle and your seat. Any greater distance makes it difficult to remain in rhythm with your horse.

LEARNING TO POST

Learning to post is best accomplished on the lunge line. With your coach controlling your horse, you can let go of the reins and focus on your horse's rhythm and your balance. By learning to post without reins, you will avoid developing the most common fault beginner riders pick up when learning to post: lifting themselves up by pulling on the reins.

Posting without stirrups is also a very effective way to learn how to post correctly. Without the stirrups it is very difficult for a rider to go up too high above the horse. In fact, if you ever wonder whether your posting is correct, kick your stirrups loose and see if anything feels different as you keep on posting. If you find yourself not rising so high, or falling down hard on the back of your horse, you were depending on your stirrups too much and your legs are too far forward. Posting without stirrups prevents you from developing another common posting fault: that of pushing up with your legs rather than letting the horse push you up in rhythm.

If you feel a double bounce as you try to post, you are probably sitting too soon. Your horse has not had the time to begin his descent when you land in the saddle. Your feet are probably too far ahead of you and your seat falls behind your base of support. Make the necessary adjustments in your position and focus on staying up longer.

Use a video recorder to see yourself as you post. Watch the tape and study your position. Are your feet directly below your seat bones as you sit in the saddle? Is the angle of your elbow opening and closing as you rise and sit? When at the apex of your flight, can you draw a straight line from your ear, through your shoulder, hip, and ankle? As you sit, feel your seat bones, thighs, and buttocks come in contact again with the suede of the saddle seat and the seat jockeys. Watch advanced riders as they post the trot on their horses. Make a very clear mental image of them as they post, then focus on that image when you try posting. See yourself looking just as they did while posting.

While posting is never required in western classes in the show ring, it is a very useful skill to apply to a warmup or conditioning trot. It is certainly useful when working a horse in the open or covering medium-range distances. Post correctly and you and your horse will benefit from the new trotting opportunities.

PART III

Aids are the means of communication between a horse and his rider. They indicate to the horse the desires of the rider and allow the rider to feel his or her mount's response, thereby ascertaining the degree to which the aids were successful.

Although the aids addressed to the horse's sense of sight play an important role in such events as cutting and roping, most aids are directed to the sense of touch. The voice and other sounds, such as the crack of the whip, are directed to the horse's well-developed sense of hearing.

A rider must have an exact understanding of the aids and their effect and must apply them at the right time with carefully measured strength. Never should a horse be afraid of the aids. For this reason all aids must take into account the degree of training, the sensitivity, and the temperament of the horse. An aid strong enough to obtain the required response with a lazy or inattentive mount could be perceived as a punishment by a more responsive horse. Hence, it is imperative that riders always be in complete control of their emotions and never let frustration or anger influence the way they apply their aids.

The aids are classified as passive and active. Aids are passive when they affect no changes in the horse's way of moving, direction of travel, speed, and frame. One example of passive aids is a rider riding across a field in a straight line, on loose reins, legs away from the horse's sides, seat neither pushing the horse nor holding him back.

Aids are active when the rider, using one aid or a combination of aids, influences the horse's natural frame, gait, body position, or direction of travel. Not all aids are necessarily active at the same time. The hands, legs, or seat—any one of them—may be passive or active, depending on the exercise requested. For instance, when turning a green colt in a circle by using the opening rein, only the rider's inside hand and lateral seat aids may be active. Should the horse slow down or lose rhythm, however, the rider may drive the horse forward with his or her seat and press with both legs, leaving only the outside hand as a passive aid.

The horse will deliver a smooth performance only when he has experienced, throughout his schooling, a very fine difference between the active and passive use of the aids. The more subtle the difference, the smoother the horse's performance. Note the subtle active hand aids (light contact) to which this horse responds by rounding his back, lowering his croup, and backing up very fast. (Photo: Ted Gard)

CHAPTER 7

The Legs, Riding Crop, Spurs, and Voice

The timely and effective application of the rider's legs to the horse's sides is essential to proper positioning of his body for optimum performance.

For centuries horsemen have discussed which is the more important aid: the legs or the hands. While it depends on the event practiced, it is safe to say that proper application of leg aids is as important as the hand aids. In their passive form the legs are completely away from the horse's sides. In their active form, the legs act, yield, or follow. Although active leg aids are very obvious when the horse is green, they become very subtle, almost invisible, as the stage approaches at which the horse's schooling is complete.

ACTING

The effectiveness of the leg aid depends very much upon the way it is applied. The method of application must be consistent and progressive, from the most subtle to the most obvious. Regardless of the purpose of your leg aids, always squeeze in a progressive manner, beginning with the upper leg and proceeding to the next most obvious action only if the response is not satisfactory. Let's ride through the sequence.

Imagine that you are riding your horse at the walk and want to move into a trot. Begin by squeezing both upper calves simultaneously. Begin with a light squeeze and increase the pressure to the maximum of your strength. Assuming that your horse does not respond to this most subtle of leg aids, squeeze your lower calves as well as your upper calves. Again, begin with light pressure and increase gradually until the horse responds or you have expended all your strength. You are now pressing with the entire length of your legs on both sides, increasing the pressure gradually. If your horse has not yet responded to your aids, press with the heels or spurs, increasing the pressure until the horse responds. The heels and spurs must be kept as aids of last recourse.

A common mistake is to bypass the progressive application of the leg, cuing the horse instead with the spurs. Since the horse is given no advanced notice of the rider's desires, the spurs are used whenever a leg aid is needed. As a result, the spur is often a surprise to the horse, creating a resentful and resistant horse.

A rider's legs assist in three very important roles. The most essential of these roles is to impart impulsion. Impulsion is paramount to correct schooling and performance. It implies that the horse is not only moving forward, but also that he is moving forward with energy and conviction. Even in such maneuvers as spins or rollbacks, the horse must be schooled with impulsion. When their role is to impart impulsion, the legs are called impulsion legs.

Another key role of the leg aids is evident during the suppling and strengthening of the horse's body through bending exercises and lateral movements. During these exercises, the rider uses his or her legs to move particular sections of the horse's body. During the execution of a lateral movement, for example, the rider's outside leg may move the horse's hindquarters to the inside of the front quarters. When the legs are used for these purposes, they are called displacing legs. A third application of leg aids is the reinforcing leg.

Impulsion Leg

To create impulsion, a rider may apply even pressure from both legs at the same time. But during the execution of lateral movements and other exercises designed to supple the horse and put him on the bit, the impulsion leg is always the one held closer to the cinch and

on the inside of the bend. The outside leg usually serves as a displacing leg. Even pressure applied from both legs at the cinch is used to drive the horse forward at the walk. Stronger pressure from both legs drives the horse forward at the trot, jog, and lope. Impulsion legs used in this way are effective also in the back up. Leg pressure should be relaxed as the horse responds.

When the legs are applied at the cinch to drive the horse forward or backward, they are said to be impulsion legs.

Displacing Leg

The displacing leg is imperative to lateral movements. It may be used to move the horse's shoulders, as in spins and cutting horse turns, in which case it is applied at the cinch. Or it may be used to move the horse's hindquarters, as in pivot on the forehand, sidepass, leg-yield, shoulder-fore, shoulder-in, half-pass, haunches-in, and flying-lead changes. In these instances, it is applied farther back on the horse's ribcage. How far back behind the cinch depends on the horse's level of training and sensitivity. As with

On green colts or dull horses, you may have to move your leg farther back than is acceptable for proper equitation. Such exaggeration of the leg position should be used only in the early stages of schooling, however.

To use a reinforcing leg properly, you must first have given a cue with the reins. Should the rein effect need reinforcement, as in turns or back ups, move your lower leg forward and bump the horse's forearm or arm with the side of the stirrup.

the impulsion legs, the displacing leg acts in a squeezing manner, yields as the horse responds, then acts again and so on until the movement is complete.

Reinforcing Leg

The reinforcing leg is not a cue. It is used only in training, to emphasize rein aids. A common application of the reinforcing leg occurs when a horse is being schooled on turn-arounds. For example, the rider effects a combination of rein aids, asking the horse to move his shoulders into a spin. The horse, uneducated or perhaps a bit sluggish, is slow to respond to the reins. The rider taps the horse's shoulder or forearm with the side of the stirrup, reinforcing the light rein effects. This leg aid is most efficient in developing the rider's ultimate goal: light, subtle, one-handed control of the horse's front quarters.

YIELDING

The yielding function of the legs is limited to relaxing the leg muscles and relieving the pressure on the horse as the mount moves away from the leg.

FOLLOWING LEG

The legs follow when they do not apply pressure during the execution of an exercise, yet remain in contact with the horse's sides after having yielded. In this position the legs assure the horse of the rider's intentions and are ready to act at the right time, if necessary. Following legs are very useful during the practice of lateral movements: the legs do not go back to a passive state again—away from the horse's sides—but rather remain in a following state in order to act and yield again until the movement is completed. To keep the leg pressure on throughout the duration of the exercise would not reward the horse for responding. The return to a passive leg indicates to the horse that the rider wants to terminate the movement. Following legs are a definite asset to the advanced rider and, together with the timely yielding of leg pressure, constitute an important key to a smooth performance.

ARTIFICIAL AIDS

Artificial aids are the instruments invented by man to reinforce the natural aids. Two artificial aids—the riding crop and the spurs—are particularly helpful in reinforcing the leg aids.

Riding Crop

The riding crop is useful for reinforcing leg and voice aids. A horse should respect the riding crop but not fear it. To this end, always precede the use of the crop with the proper application of the natural aids. Then, if necessary, use the crop in a measured, authoritative manner. If the horse fears the crop, training sessions will not be as productive as they should be because his attention will rest, not with the aids you want him to learn, but rather with the crop.

Spurs

Spurs are an artificial aid used to reinforce leg cues. Unfortunately, they are often looked upon as an ornament, part of the cowboy's uniform. This fantasy causes many riders to abuse their horses through the misuse of spurs.

One of the most widespread misconceptions about spurs is that they will make a horse run faster. To truly grasp the depth of this error, picture yourself running a sprint race. Someone running beside you carries a spur and, with every stride you take, jabs you in the ribs with

it. You quickly lose your desire to even approach the track. The same result occurs when horses are worked by spur-happy riders. They become dull to the leg and spur, show their displeasure by wringing their tails, and eventually resent training to the point that they perform as little as possible. Spurring a young horse too early in training makes him afraid of the rider's legs. Such misuse results in jerky movements and nervousness.

When should the spurs be used? When the horse thoroughly understands the maneuver but needs to sharpen its execution. Even then, a horse must be given the opportunity to respond crisply without feeling the spurs. The rider should first apply a light, subtle cue with the leg. If the horse needs more encouragement, leg pressure is increased until the spur touches the horse. The pressure applied with the spur is also increased until the horse responds in the desired manner. Leading with a light leg cue guarantees a horse who will respond in a soft fashion. Increasing the leg pressure prior to using the spur gives the horse ample opportunity to respond before the reinforcement occurs. When such progression is used, the spur is never abusive to the horse. It is, however, very disruptive to the horse's mind when a rider, giving his mount no specific cue, jabs the spurs in the horse's ribs. Such action denotes a great lack of horsemanship.

When using the spur, the rider must consider its sharpness and the sensitivity of the horse. The rider should never use spurs with such force that they draw blood, and their application must cease the instant the horse responds. Riders must never forget that the spurs, whether used as a punishment or as an aid, are the last resort. Spurs should not be used by riders who cannot control their tempers.

Spurs are important instruments that can make a horse truly excel in negotiating the maneuvers he has already mastered. Only accomplished riders should wear them, for only they have the independent seat and aids that result in the stability of the lower leg needed for proper timing in the use of spurs.

VOICE

The human voice is a very effective tool in training horses for all sorts of events. As with all aids, its use is most obvious when working with green horses. Four to five sessions of lungeing while using your voice will suffice to get the horse to understand basic commands. Voice cues can also be taught by simply leading the horse, or while riding.

There are great benefits to teaching a horse basic voice commands during ground work. You will be able to remain very light with your hands if the colt understands the significance of the word "whoa." And you will not have to surprise a green colt with your legs if, even before he is ever ridden, the mount associates a kissing sound with forward motion. By varying the tone of your voice and the rhythm at which it is used, you can teach a horse such commands as walk, trot, lope, stop, or back.

When using your voice for upward transitions, speak in an authoritative tone and emphasize the end of the spoken command. For downward transitions, speak softly, in a soothing tone.

School horses, in particular, must understand voice commands. Such understanding is of primary importance because the instructor should be able to control the horse from a distance.

The voice is essential to the trainer in developing a performance horse. As schooling progresses, the voice is often replaced by the more subtle actions of the other natural aids.

CHAPTER 8

The Seat

The seat must remain centered on the horse, even when the lateral seat aids are applied to the maximum.

The seat aids are defined by the manner in which the rider places his or her weight in the saddle. This manner varies according to the gait at which the horse travels, the direction of the movement, and the effect desired.

Of all the aids, the seat is the most important, yet the most misunderstood. It is the most misunderstood because it is not as easily demonstrated and as obvious to a learner as the leg and hand aids. It is the most important because together with the thighs it is the rider's connection with the horse's back, the most important link between the hindquarters and the mouth. So influential is the rider's seat to the horse's performance that any modification of the rider's weight placement in the saddle changes the center of gravity of the horse-rider team. Hence, the fluid, relaxed, and complete contact of the deep seat to the horse's back, regardless of the gait travelled, is key to the timely application of the aids for the execution of all maneuvers. In fact, the seat aids will be ineffective and even contradictory to the other aids unless a rider develops those characteristic of the independent seat outlined in chapter 4.

The seat is said to be passive when the rider lets the horse move him or her. The rider's muscles are relaxed and his or her back and weight are divided evenly on both seat bones. At all times during the stride, the rider does not aid the horse into any lengthening or shortening of stride, lateral movement, increase in speed, or stop.

The seat is active when, by contracting certain muscle groups or by taking specific positions, the rider influences the horse's stride or the direction of

Your seat is potentially the most subtle, most powerful, and most effective aid at your disposal.

travel. The active seat can influence the horse's stride by driving the horse forward with energy, in which case it is called the driving seat. The active seat can also influence the horse's stride by slowing it down or shortening it. In this instance it is called a holding seat. Lastly, the active seat can influence the horse's direction of travel when the rider places more weight on one seat bone than on the other. (This use of the active seat aids is discussed in the section on lateral seat aids.) The seat aids are effective only when used in tandem with the leg and hand aids. For this reason, the use of the legs and hands as they apply to seat aids is integrated into the discussion. Since the use of seat aids varies according to the gait ridden, I will discuss them in terms of a specific gait.

AT THE WALK

The walk is a four-beat gait during which each foot touches the ground independently during

every stride. Since the movement of each foot affects the movement of the horse's back, the saddle moves more at the walk than at the trot or lope. The sequence of footfall for one complete stride is as follows: if the horse begins with the right hind, it is followed by the right front, then the left hind, and finally the left front. As the horse brings the right hind forward, he pushes with the left hind and his belly and his back swing forward and to the left. His left hip is lower than his right hip, leaving the right side of

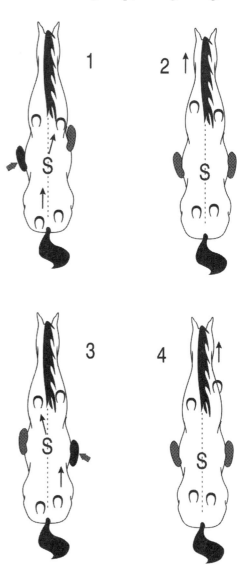

To increase the length of stride at the walk, drive the horse with your seat and leg on the same side as the hind limb in flight—beats one and three of the four-beat walk stride. Note the passive aids in beats two and four.

his ribcage higher than the left side. Before his right hind touches the ground, his right front lifts off to begin the second beat of the stride. Then the same movements are repeated to the left for the third and fourth beat of the stride, and so on.

Passive Seat

Much of what you feel through your seat is directly related to the movement of the horse's hind limbs. Feel your right seat bone rise slightly higher than the left seat bone as the horse's right hip rises to allow the right hind to come forward and the left hip lowers as the horse pushes on his left hind. Then the saddle follows the horse's back and swings forward, to the right, and rises slightly under the left seat bone as the left hind lifts off the ground and begins the flight forward for the third beat of the walk stride. The movement of the front limbs—beats two and four of the stride—have little perceptible effect on the saddle. As the horse's back swings to the left when he pushes with the left hind, so do your legs. Feel your right leg drawn into the horse's right side as he lifts the right hind and pushes with the left hind. Alternately, feel your left leg being drawn to the horse's side as he lifts the left hind and pushes with the right hind. In summary, the passive seat goes forward and to the right with the left leg "pulled into" the horse as he pushes with the right hind. Then forward and to the left with the right leg "pulled into" the horse as he pushes with the left hind, and so on. It is important that riders feel each beat if they are to use their aids effectively.

Driving Seat

To drive the horse, use a combination of seat and leg. As the saddle begins to move forward and slightly right, tighten your abdominal muscles and "send the saddle over the horse's withers" while at the same time applying pressure with the left leg. Then momentarily relax the muscles and follow the horse's back. Then tighten up the muscles and apply right-leg pressure as the saddle moves forward and to the left,

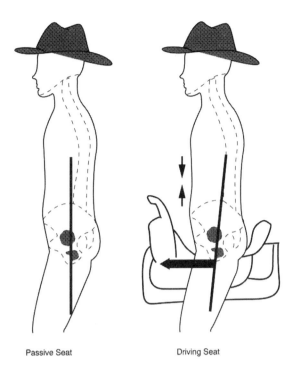

Passive Seat   Driving Seat

Your abdominal muscles play a key role in driving the horse forward at the walk and lope. The momentary contraction of these muscles draws your pelvis and sternum closer to each other and results in a quick and brief thrusting forward of your seat bones. The vertical axis from the ischial tuberosity (see chapt. 4) to the hip slopes backward slightly as "you push the saddle over the horse's withers." Your upper body should remain upright.

and so on. When the thrust of the seat bones and the pressure from the leg are applied in rhythm with the forward flight of each hind leg, the result is a deeper engagement of the horse's hind legs, a longer stride, and a faster pace. To create the desired round back and elevation of the frontquarters, establish soft contact with the horse's mouth as you drive him with your seat and legs. The light restraint on the horse's mouth will channel some of the forward energy upward, resulting in elevation of the rib cage.

Holding Seat

The holding seat may be used to shorten the stride and slow the pace, or it may be used as an aid in stopping the horse. To shorten the stride and slow down the rhythm, tighten your lower back and stomach muscles and immobilize your hips. Maintain this intentional tension in the muscles until the horse responds and shortens the stride. As you hold this tension, make contact with the horse's mouth and squeeze your legs on his sides. The holding seat, leg pressure, and hand aids must be coordinated in a manner that allows for a downward transition during which the horse remains forward and responsive to the aids. If the purpose of the holding seat is to stop the horse, keep your legs off the horse's sides and coordinate your holding seat with slow, steady hands. Be careful not to tighten up the buttocks and adductor muscles, since this would drive your seat out of the saddle and cause your horse not to feel the differences in your seat aids.

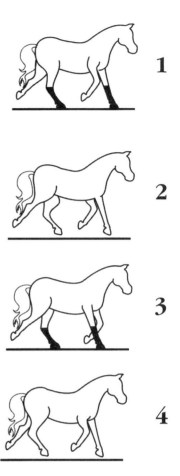

The jog and trot. In figures 1 and 3, the horse's diagonal legs have landed and his back is at the lowest point of the stride. Figures 2 and 4 show the horse in suspension with his back at the crest of the rise.

AT THE TROT

The trot is a two-beat gait during which the horse moves his feet in a diagonal fashion: right front–left hind is one beat, left front–right hind is the other beat. In between each beat the horse is in suspension and his back is at the highest point of the stride. When the diagonal feet touch the ground, your horse's body is at the lowest point of the stride. Therefore the horse's back rises and lowers twice for each stride, sending the saddle straight up and down. At the sitting trot, you must follow with soft contact of your seat. Any bouncing you fail to absorb with your body is transmitted to your shoulders, arms, and hands. The result is bouncy hands, which cause pain to the horse's mouth and produce a stiff horse.

Passive Seat

In chapter 6 I explained that because your body is considerably lighter than your horse's body, and you are pushed up and forward with the same force that pushes him up and forward, you stay in the air longer than he does. The chart showed how you make contact with the saddle as he begins his next ascent. This contact of your descending body and the ascending saddle is the source of the jolt you feel when sitting the trot. In chapter 4 we studied the muscles at the back of the thigh. Through their ability to pull the seat bones downward, these muscles are helpful in sitting in balance at the trot. Here I will explain how this process is achieved.

To follow the up-and-down movements of the horse's back, relax your hip joints and push your thigh, knee, and heel toward the ground when the horse's back is at its lowest. Alternate between the left leg and the right leg every time your descending seat meets the ascending saddle. Since your leg cannot be made longer, pushing your left heel closer to the ground results in the biceps femoris, the semimembranosus, and the semitendinosus pulling your left seat bone into the saddle. The relaxed muscles of your thigh absorb the shock of meeting the ascending saddle and thus let you stay closer to the saddle on the next push up and forward. The result is a subtle tipping of your hips to the right and then to the left.

To help achieve this lateral tipping of the pelvis to the right and then to the left, pretend that your legs are loaded with oranges. Each time the horse's back is at its lowest point, drop an orange from your heel by jerking your leg down. When you first start doing this, exaggerate the movement to help identify the correct feel. Then let the upward movement of the horse's back close your hip and fill your buttocks with the saddle. Your head and shoulders should remain level and relaxed. With this method of sitting the trot your leg and hip joint absorb the jolts of the horse's back.

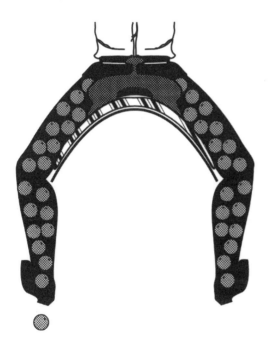

The relaxation and stretching of the hip joint muscles—such as adductors and gluteus maximus—are key to bounceless sitting at the trot. Picture your legs heavy with oranges; as the horse's back reaches the lowest point of the stride, feel one of your thighs stretch in the hip joint and gently shake an orange down from your heel.

Driving Seat

To drive the horse with your seat, tighten your lower back muscles and push your leg down even harder at the moment when the horse's spine is at its lowest point during the stride. This gives the horse a feeling of increased weight from your seat bones. The increased weight pushes the horse's spine farther down, and providing you relax your muscles immediately as his spine begins its upward swing, the increase in downward swing will be balanced by an increase in upward swing. The higher upward swing enables the horse to bring his hind legs deeper under himself for a more engaged or longer stride. Driving the horse while on loose reins will result in a faster gait. If you want to lower the croup and elevate the frontquarters, establish contact with his mouth as you drive him forward with your seat and legs.

The same principle applies to the rising trot. Since you sit as the horse's back is on the downswing, drive him forward by pushing gently after you make soft contact with the saddle. Squeeze your legs on the horse as you sit to encourage deeper engagement of the hind legs or a faster pace. A word of caution: do not drive the horse with your seat until he is conditioned and has built some strength in his back muscles. To sit heavier on the back of a colt or an out-of-condition horse would only serve to sore his back and hollow it out rather than promote roundness and deeper engagement.

Holding Seat

To restrain the action of the horse's back and hind legs, tighten your abdominal and lower back muscles momentarily—not the gluteus maximus—when the undulating movement of the horse's back begins the upswing phase of the beat. This tightening of the muscles immobilizes your pelvis. Your stiff midsection makes it more difficult for the horse to swing his back so high and thereby reduce his capacity to travel so fast or long. To curb the action of the horse's back at the rising trot, allow a slight delay before you begin to rise out of the saddle. This pause puts pressure on the horse's back as it begins its upward swing, thus reducing its amplitude of movement. As with the walk, if the purpose of the holding seat is to slow the pace or change gait, leg pressure and contact with the mouth need to be applied to maintain

Avoid the hollow lower back (top) or the round back (bottom). Both result in a rotated pelvis and take away the ability of the pelvis and hip joints to follow the up-and-down movements of the horse's back.

forward motion and responsiveness. If the purpose is to stop the horse, combine your holding seat aids with a slow pick up of the reins until you feel the soft contact of the horse's mouth.

AT THE LOPE

The lope is a three-beat gait. When he lopes on the right lead, the horse's feet land in this sequence: left hind lands and pushes the horse forward; right hind and left fore land at the same time and then the leading right front. Then comes a moment of suspension before the left hind touches down again. During this foot work, the horse's back tilts up and down like a teeter-totter.

Passive Seat

To follow the motion of the horse's back, allow the front of your body to stretch and your lower back to hollow slightly as the horse's back tips down. Then let the horse shorten the front of your body and close your hips as his back tips up. Keep the muscles of your thighs and buttocks relaxed to allow the horse to round his back and move his hind legs freely during the movement of suspension. Relaxed thighs and buttocks also let your seat bones slide back and forth inside your skin—a key to absorbing the movements of the horse's back. This means that the seat of your pants never moves from its proper placement in the saddle. And it means that the movement necessary for proper riding of each lope stride depends upon the degree of relaxation in your midsection and hip joints.

Driving Seat

You can best drive the horse with your seat when his back is tipped down. At this precise moment the horse's hind feet are off the ground and he can still alter their action. To be effective at the right time, tighten your lower stomach muscles and thrust the saddle forward at the beginning of the downswing. Just as with

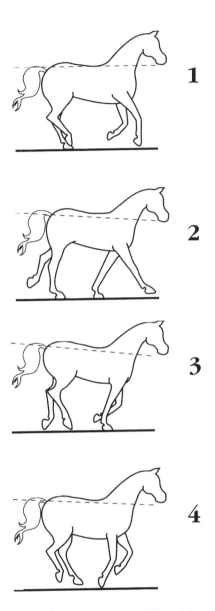

1

2

3

4

The horse's back is at its most uphill position during the first beat of the stride, when the outside hind leg lands and pushes the horse forward (1). It tips down during the second beat of the stride as the diagonal legs touch the ground (2). It is at its lowermost position when the lead fore lands (3), after which it tips up again during the moment of suspension (4).

the walk, try to push the saddle onto the horse's withers with your pelvis. Be sure not to push with your shoulders. This serious riding fault is made obvious by an upper body that tilts back and forth. Aside from being ineffective at driving the horse forward, pushing with the shoulders causes much stiffness in your upper body. This stiffness causes your seat to come out of the sad-

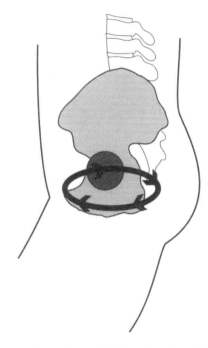

Keep your buttocks and thighs relaxed to allow your seat bones to slide back and forth within your skin. Imagine each seat bone (ischial ramus) drawing an oval. As the horse's back tips down, the seat bones draw the lower segment of the oval. As the horse's back levels out during the moment of suspension, the seat bones draw the front of the oval. As the horse pushes with the outside hind leg, the seat bones draw the top and rear part of the oval, and so on, stride after stride. When riding a circle, the outside seat bone draws a bigger oval than the inside seat bone.

dle and your hands to bounce and hurt the horse's mouth. The consequence is a hollow-backed, short-strided, stiff horse who is unable to perform to his full potential, whatever his speciality.

Holding Seat

To slow the pace, tighten your stomach and back muscles during the moment of upswing and suspension. The extra weight communicated to the horse's back will prevent him from rounding his back and, consequently, drive the hind legs into the ground for a shorter stride. Once again, if your purpose in applying the holding seat is to ride from a gallop to a lope, for instance, you must coordinate leg and hand aids to maintain forward impulsion and prevent the horse from loosing his frame, stretching out,

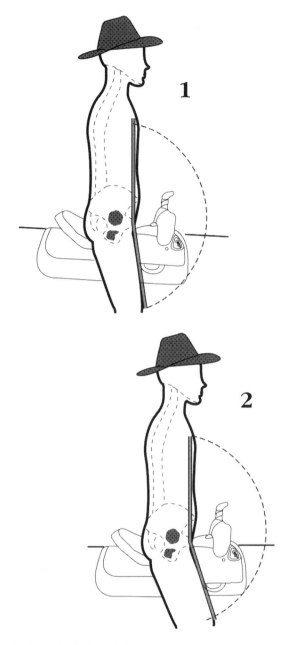

In figure 1, the horse's back is at its downmost tilt. To absorb this movement, the rider has let the front of her body stretch and the small of her back hollow slightly. As a result, the angle between her upper body and her thigh has opened up. In figure 2, the horse's back has leveled out and the rider lets the front of her body shorten. The angle between her upper body and her thigh has closed. Notice that her upper body constantly remains at a ninety-degree angle to the ground.

and falling apart. If your intent is to stop the horse, keep your legs away from the horse and slowly lift the slack out of the reins. (For more information about stops, see chapt. 16.)

LEARNING TO USE YOUR SEAT AIDS

Initial learning of the seat aids is best done while the horse is on the lunge line. Thus, the rider need not think about guiding the horse and can concentrate on the feel of each gait and the timing of the aids. Practice your skills at applying passive, driving, and holding seat aids at the walk, trot, and lope until you feel a distinct muscular effort when contracting and releasing lower-back and stomach muscles. In the beginning, ride without stirrups and stretch your arms above your head to increase the feel in your seat. Ride four or five strides passive, then four or five strides driving, then hold for a few strides, change the order of the aids, and try again.

LATERAL SEAT AIDS

A horse's narrow transversal base of support makes him sensitive to the lateral shift of the rider's weight. Therefore, the proper location of the rider's center of gravity has the potential to greatly facilitate or hinder the horse's balance and his ability to perform the required maneuver. It is impossible to give hard rules as to how to achieve harmonious balance. No two human beings are balanced the same; neither are two horses. It is, however, possible to note some general principles that may help. We know that the horse moves his center of gravity toward the direction of his bending. We know also that the horse moves his center of gravity left or right to remain under the rider's center of gravity. Therefore, when the horse is bent in the desired fashion and moving in the direction of the bend, the rider's inside seat bone should be weighted slightly more than the outside one. Exceptions to this general rule are spins and rollbacks. In these two maneuvers the horse must maintain a stationary pivot with his inside hind leg but also has to move his inside front limb laterally in the direction of the turn. Placing the weight to the inside hinders the

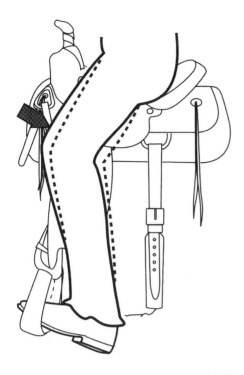

To place more weight on one seat bone, drive the knee on the same side toward the ground while keeping your upper body straight.

Any lateral shift of weight must be very subtle if it is to benefit rather than hinder your horse's performance. Your seat must remain centered on your horse even when you apply your lateral seat aids to the maximum.

horse's ability to move the inside front limb and shoulder into the turn and forces him to swing his hindquarters out.

When the desired bend is opposite to the direction of travel, the rider should place more weight in the direction of travel to facilitate the movement by inciting the horse to move his center of gravity in the direction of travel.

Lateral work demands more of the horse than other straightforward exercises. Because of this higher degree of difficulty, its benefits to the horse's overall ability to perform are tremendous. However, if the horse's muscle structure is to benefit from the exercises, the rider must ensure that the horse is moving forward with impulsion at all times during the movement. Consequently, the rider must, in addition to the weighting of one seat bone more than the other, apply a driving seat throughout the exercise to maintain impulsion.

Any shifting that is easily noticeable to an onlooker is exaggerated and inefficient. Riders who lean one way or the other when performing such exercises as sidepass, two-track, leg-yield, or half-pass hinder their horse's performance and show a weak seat. Their legs are less effective than those of riders whose strong independent seat anchors them well into place for powerful and timely leg aids.

CHAPTER 9

The Hands

Every time you make contact with the horse's mouth you either develop relaxation and responsiveness or fear and resistance.

Knowledgeable hands—the most important tools for handling horses—are essential to successful horsemanship. The trainer's hands control the bit or the bosal. They reward the horse.

Like other aids, the hands are either passive or active. The passive hand has no contact with the horse's mouth and effects no changes in the horse's body position or direction of travel. By means of the bit the active hand influences all of the horse's actions by acting, yielding, holding, and following. Through various combinations of these actions experienced riders can bring their horses to perform graceful exercises at various speeds.

ACTING

The hands act by applying pressure to the bit in a lateral or rearward direction according to any of the rein effects described later in this chapter. Such action can be used to change the direction of travel, slow down, stop, back up, or put the horse on the bit.

All actions of the hands should be slow. If you are riding on loose reins, you should first establish contact with the horse's mouth, then indicate your intentions to the horse. Jerking the reins only serves to scare him and cause him to stiffen and resist.

When riding with two hands, hold the reins with the thumbs on top. This position allows for better feel and more supple wrist joints, which let your hands "breathe with the horse's mouth." Ride with your hands just above the swells. Keep them six to eight inches apart to maintain straightness in your horse and prepare him for times when you ride with one hand.

Do not hold the hands with the knuckles on top. This position causes a twisting of the two bones in the forearm and reduces the sensitivity and responsiveness of the hands. Held in this position the wrist bends little and cannot follow the horse's mouth for the soft, steady contact that builds relaxation in the horse's body.

The horse must respect the bit but not fear it. To progress in training and perform properly, your horse must be able to trust you. He must know that your hands will never hurt his mouth. Your horse's mouth should never be hurt because of your misunderstandings and inappropriate riding habits.

YIELDING

The moment the horse responds to your asking hands, open the fingers slightly and release the tension on the reins. This is called yielding.

Yielding is very important since it is the only indication you can give your horse that he has responded properly to the command. It is your horse's reward. This reward must be simultaneous with the end of the response, rather than given after the horse has responded. Many a heavy-mouthed and stiff-jawed horse has been made that way because of unyielding hands.

HOLDING

The hands must hold when the horse does not respond to their action and tries to evade the aids. To hold effectively, tighten your fingers and your wrist, elbow, and shoulder joints. This stiffening of your arm immobilizes your hand in a specific spot. Your hand neither yields nor pulls. Your horse comes against the solidity of your hand and pushes against it to test whether he can avoid performing the exercise required of him.

Timely holding is key to horsemanship. If a rider does not know when and how to hold, the horse will know that evasion is possible. A great lesson of discipline and lightness can be taught to the horse when the rider holds and then yields at the very instant the horse relaxes his jaw and flexes at the poll.

It is important to understand the difference between pulling and holding. A pull is a continual drawing toward you of your hand. A pulling hand continues to take after the horse has given to the action. Pulling occurs when riders use their biceps and forearm muscles to hold. Proper holding is done through the use of the upper back muscles in combination with the triceps.

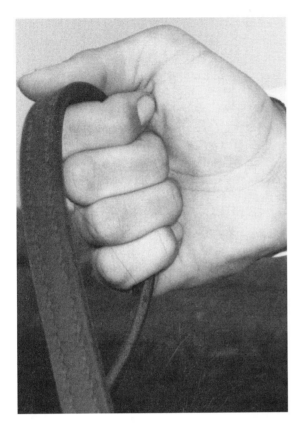

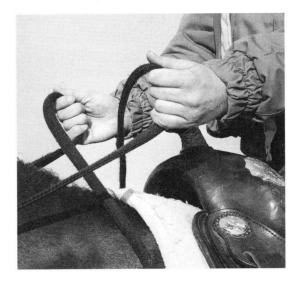

If you ride with split reins, cross them over the horse's withers.

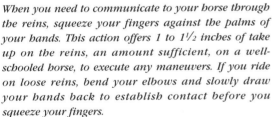

When you need to communicate to your horse through the reins, squeeze your fingers against the palms of your hands. This action offers 1 to 1½ inches of take up on the reins, an amount sufficient, on a well-schooled horse, to execute any maneuvers. If you ride on loose reins, bend your elbows and slowly draw your hands back to establish contact before you squeeze your fingers.

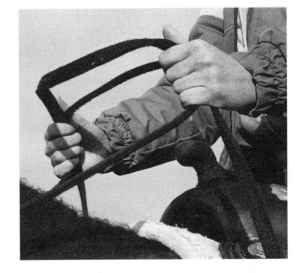

Do not hold the reins in a bridge. The extra reins going through your hands make it difficult to be as light and sensitive as you should be with your fingers.

FOLLOWING

Although a measure of specialized riding is done on loose reins, the ability to enhance the performance of the competition horse is greatly increased when the rider can school the horse "on the bit," or "on the bridle," as is also said.

The challenge in schooling a horse on the bit comes from the fact that the horse's head is never completely still while he moves, particularly at the walk and lope. To keep the horse on the bit, the rider's hands must follow the horse's mouth. This skill, also referred to as letting your hands "breathe with the horse's mouth," is essential in developing or maintaining

The three-rein position allows for a quick shortening of the inside rein if the schooling situation calls for such action.

a balanced and sensitive horse. To ride with still hands and not follow the horse's mouth will cause the horse to jerk his mouth on the bit every time his head comes forward and down when a particular gait requires him to do that for balance.

The term "steady hands" is often employed during horsemanship lessons. Yet it is misleading since it implies that the rider's hands do not move. In fact, the hands *must* follow the horse's mouth. Following is achieved by relaxing the shoulders, elbows, and wrists. The elbow joint, the most important of the three, opens and closes considerably to allow the hands to follow the movement of the horse's head.

To better understand how your elbow joints should work when you ride a horse on the bit, hold one of the reins in each hand. Have a friend hold the bit in his or her hands and move it back and forth between you a distance of about six or seven inches. Be sure your upper body remains still and maintain a light contact on the bit as it is moved back and forth between you and your friend. Feel how your shoulder joints move slightly and see how much your elbow joints must open and close to keep a soft contact with your friend's hands through the reins and bit.

Now mount your horse. Begin at the walk on loose reins and observe how much your horse moves his head. Once you have a clear idea of the rhythm of his head movements, shorten the reins and establish a light contact with his mouth. Relax your arms and let the horse open and close your elbow and shoulder joints in rhythm with the balancing movements of his head. It is natural for the rider to try to follow the mouth by physically opening and closing these joints. This is not a good practice since the beginner cannot follow the rhythm and eventually pulls and jerks on the horse's mouth. It is better to focus on the elastic feeling of the horse's mouth and try to maintain contact with it through relaxation of the joints.

At the trot the horse's head does not move; therefore, your hands will follow if they do not bounce. At the sitting trot, a good seat ensures that your hands do not bounce. At the rising trot your elbow joints must open and close so your hands can remain steady while your upper body goes up and down. A good way to develop this skill is to rest your little fingers on the swells of the saddle as you rise and sit. Feel your elbows open and close and then try to do it without resting your fingers on the swells.

At the lope the horse extends his neck and lowers his head as his back tilts down, shortening his neck and raising his head as his back tilts up. Nurture the elastic feeling in your hands by relaxing your arms so that they can follow the horse's head on the way down and take up the slack on the way up.

A firm, secure, independent seat is paramount to these hand actions, which are basic to proper horsemanship. Unless the motion of the horse is absorbed by your hip joints, knees, ankles, and lower back, your shoulders will jump. This in turn results in bouncing hands. Their pulls and jerks will cause a horse to stiffen in an attempt to get away from the pain.

REIN EFFECTS

The rein effects act directly on the horse's head, neck, and shoulders, positioning these parts of the horse's body to enable him to better negotiate various maneuvers.

Regardless of the action of the hands, however, rein effects are effective only when impulsion, or forward motion, is maintained. Therefore, the rider should never underestimate the importance of the leg aids in maintaining a responsive horse. In fact, a horse remains responsive to the rein effects only when the rider uses the other aids to the fullest extent.

Opening Rein

The opening or leading rein is used in the early stages of training any horse. As its name implies, it literally leads the horse's nose and the rest of his body along a turn. The opening rein gets its name from the rider's hand opening the angle between the horse's neck and the rein. Because of its natural action, this effect is very helpful in schooling a horse who has not yet learned to respond to other rein effects.

Aside from its simplicity of use, the opening rein has many advantages. It does not discourage the green horse from maintaining the same speed, or cadence, as he turns. A colt is likely to slow down or break gait if a direct rein or an indirect rein of opposition is used to cue him into a turn. Later in training, after the horse has learned to respond to leg aids and lateral seat aids, he can be weaned from the leading rein.

To a beginning rider, the opening rein is very easy to use. To apply a right opening rein, move your right hand to the right, gently pulling the horse's nose in that direction. Never pull down toward your knee or up toward your shoulder. Rather, move your inside or active hand in an imaginary line parallel to the ground.

Any snaffle bit is suitable for opening rein effects. Do not effect an opening rein when a curb bit is in your horse's mouth. The action of your hand will cause the bit to twist in his mouth, resulting in injury or fear.

Direct Rein of Opposition

The direct rein of opposition is useful when you ride horses at the intermediate and advanced levels of schooling. Although it applies a more subtle cue than the opening rein, its effect is similar: the horse bends and turns in the direction of the pull. The direct rein can be used as a reinforcement of the neck rein or as the main rein effect during the execution of small circles and turns. Simultaneous application of a left and right direct rein brings the horse to a downward transition, a stop, or a back up.

Snaffle bits, bosals, side-pulls, and loose-jaw curb bits are suitable for use of the direct rein.

Neck Rein

The neck rein is a learned rein effect. In response to the neck rein, the well-schooled horse moves his forequarters away from the rein as he bends his neck very slightly in the direction of the turn. The neck rein is often required in the show ring and necessary in working situations in which the rider must use one hand for roping or leading a pack string.

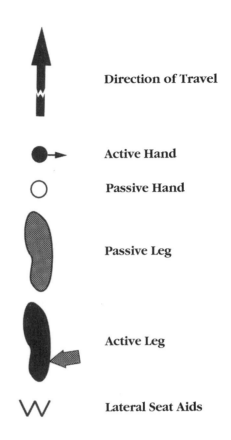

Direction of Travel

Active Hand

Passive Hand

Passive Leg

Active Leg

Lateral Seat Aids

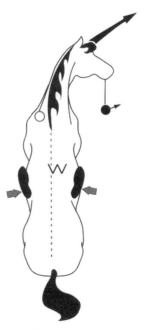

Opening rein to the right: (1) The right hand is active, moving to the right; (2) the left hand is passive, yielding forward and low; (3) the legs act to maintain impulsion and pace if the horse slows down; (4) the weight shifts to the right seat bone; (5) the horse bends and turns right.

The opening rein's name comes from the angle the rider's hand opens between the horse's neck and the rein.

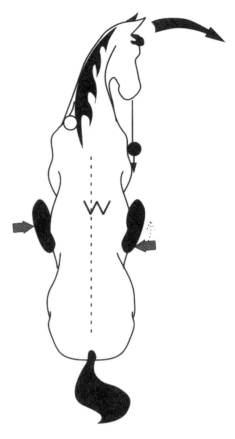

Direct rein of opposition to the right: (1) The right hand moves parallel to the horse's body toward the rider's hip; (2) the left hand is passive and serves in a give-and-take fashion to regulate the amount of bend in the horse's neck; (3) leg aids bend the horse's body and maintain balance and impulsion; (4) the inside seat bone carries slightly more weight than the outside one; (5) the horse's nose comes to the right and back slightly, his inside shoulder bears more weight than the other quarters, and he bends and turns to the right.

To effect a direct rein of opposition, apply pressure to the horse's mouth by moving your hand toward your hip.

Although pressure on the horse's mouth is necessary to school the horse to respond to the neck rein, the finished horse responds to pressure on his neck as light as that of the weight of the rein.

In the process of schooling the horse to the neck rein, apply the outside rein to his neck and indicate the desired response to him through the application of an opening rein, a displacing leg to the ribs, or a reinforcing leg to the arm or forearm.

Take care not to cross the mane line with your neck rein hand. During such faulty application, the neck rein and bit exert a strong pull on the outside of the horse's mouth. The result is

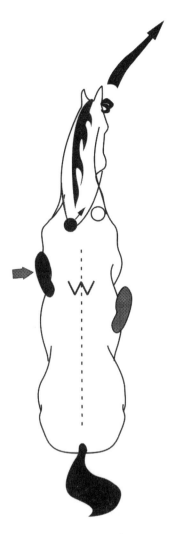

Neck rein to the right:(1) Left rein applies light pressure on the left side of the horse's neck; (2) The horse slightly bends his body in the direction of the turn and moves away from the rein.

This horse moves away from the light touch of the rein on the middle of her neck. There is definite slack in the reins. (Photo: Ted Gard)

Indirect Rein of Opposition

The inderect rein of opposition is useful in schooling the western performance horse at the intermediate and advanced levels. It serves well to position a horse on the circle or to straighten a crooked horse. It is an important rein effect when schooling the cutting horse. Cutting horse riders use the indirect rein of opposition to bend the horse's body and keep the horse's shoulders from falling in toward the cow when riding parallel to it.

Since this rein effect displaces much of the horse's weight from one shoulder to the other, it is important to use a sufficiently strong leg at the cinch to prevent the horse from resisting your hands.

Avoid crossing the mane line with the active hand because doing so causes the horse's neck to twist and results in a loss of vertical balance. If the horse is sluggish in his response, reinforce the rein effect with your leg on the same side: right hand with right leg or left hand with left leg.

a horse forced to turn with his neck twisted, his nose to the outside of the turn, and his shoulder falling in the circle. Instead of crossing the mane line and pulling on the neck rein when the horse does not respond, reinforce the cue with your inside hand and outside leg.

Proper use of the indirect rein of opposition in front of the withers builds shoulder control and develops suppleness in the front quarters.

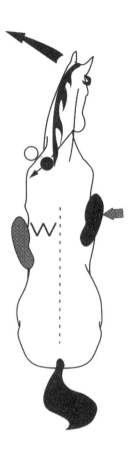

Right indirect rein of opposition: (1) The right hand moves toward the back and the left side of the horse, in front of the withers; (2) The left hand yields and regulates the amount of flexion in the neck; (3) The left leg maintains impulsion; (4) The right leg acts at the cinch to assist the right hand in pushing the shoulders to the left; (5) The weight shifts to the left; (6) The horse's nose comes to the right and back, his neck flexes to the right, and much of his weight moves to his left shoulder as he turns left.

PART IV

Communication is the key to understanding and the basis of performance. Much of the communication between a rider and his mount flows through the bit and enters the horse's mind by way of his mouth. For this reason it is not surprising that in the centuries since the domestication of the horse, countless careers have been devoted to the design and fitting of bits. These bits have ranged from the mildest possible form to cruel instruments of torture. While the designs have changed, the principles upon which bits act have not changed much. The two most common and useful types of bits employed today are the snaffle bit and the curb bit. In this part of the book I detail the many variations of each type and explain how they act in the horse's mouth. I comment on the severity of each design, keeping in mind that this assessment is only comparative, since I have no way of knowing how you use your hands with any type of bit. Above all, the rider's hands are the factor that most influences the severity or softness of a bit. Soft and slow hands combined with seat and leg aids can turn any bit into an exquisite tool of suggestive communication. Hard hands, however, will injure the horse's mouth even when the mildest of bits is used. There are no bits designed to overcome bad hands.

Parallel to the development of bits, horsemen have invented instruments to help them maximize the bits and aids. The foundational designs of these bitting instruments are centuries old. Their correct use has proven their effectiveness on thousands and thousands of horses, whatever their type or function. A dangerous dependency on these instruments nevertheless awaits the rider and horse who use them too much. However, since you cannot become a complete horseman without an understanding of the purpose of these instruments and an awareness of the potential damage caused by their misuse, I include a chapter on their applications and encourage you to familiarize yourself with them.

Before I get into the mechanics of bits and bitting, let's look at the horse's mouth and some possible causes of bitting problems.

A horse's mouth has twelve incisors in the front and twenty-four to twenty-eight molars in the back. The two groups of teeth are separated by an interdental space. In this interdental space, called the bars, grow the canine teeth and the wolf teeth. Canine teeth are the tusklike teeth that grow next to the incisors. Wolf teeth, shallow-rooted teeth that grow next to the molars, usually appear when the horse is between two and one half and three years old and should be removed as soon as you can feel them poking through the gums. Since the mouthpiece of the snaffle bit can bump these teeth, failure to remove them often leads to head tossing.

Between the right and left bars is a concave area that serves as the tongue channel. In the adult horse it generally measures between $1^1/_4$ inches and $1^1/_2$ inches wide and $1^1/_2$ inches deep. The channel is wide enough but not deep enough to accommodate the tongue, so the tongue is higher than the bars. These observations are important: any mouthpiece with a port whose base is wider than $1^1/_2$ inches will not contact the sides of the tongue. If the port is at least $1^1/_2$ inches high, the mouthpiece does not utilize the tongue as a point of contact. A port any lower than this puts pressure on the top of the tongue but not on the sides.

The bit lies in the area of the bars, approximately two inches below the first molars. Sensitivity in the bars, tongue, and corners of the lips varies greatly from horse to horse. As a rule, a horse with a fleshy, fatty head is not as responsive to the bit as one who has well-defined head features.

The upper jaw features the hard palate, which extends from the incisors in the front all the way to the back of the molars. Covered by ridges of soft tissue, the hard palate is very sensitive to the high ports of some curb bits. The shallower the palate, or roof of the horse's mouth, the more sensitive the horse will be to the bit.

The tongue is a large muscle covered with epithelial cells that are very sensitive, adding to the horse's responsiveness to bit pressure.

Care must be taken to maintain the horse's mouth in bitting condition. I have already said that the wolf teeth should be pulled as soon as they appear. The upper molars deserve special attention also. Because the upper molars are wider than the lower ones, their sharp surface often causes sores on the inside of the horse's mouth. These sores are aggravated by the halter, noseband, or cheek pieces of the bit as they touch and press on the horse's cheeks. Consequently, a number of horses are driven to resistance in an effort to escape the pain. Avoid possible bitting problems by having your veterinarian or equine dentist float your horse's teeth at least once a year.

Regular examination of your horse's mouth and proper care of his teeth can help avoid a number of bitting problems. Once you are certain your horse's mouth is in good condition, you can focus your efforts on the equipment you use and the way you use it. Your horse, if not preoccupied by sore cheeks or a bit hitting his teeth, will show signs of well-being as he learns the correct response to your aids.

CHAPTER 10

Snaffle Bits

When it comes to bits, less is more.

A snaffle is a nonleverage bit that exerts a direct pull from the mouthpiece to the rider's hands as contact is made with the horse's mouth. The mouthpiece may be jointed or solid. It acts primarily on the horse's tongue but on the corners of the mouth as well, and depending on the type of bit used and the rein effect employed, the snaffle bit may also act on the sides of the horse's mouth. The commonly held belief that a jointed snaffle acts as a nutcracker when pressure is applied on both reins is wrong. Research has shown that equal force on both reins causes uniform pressure across the entire width of the tongue.

CHEEK PIECES

The reins attach to the mouthpiece by means of various cheek pieces, also called rings, or side pieces. There are two families of cheek pieces: those whose rings are loose and rotate up and down (as well as left to right at the joint with the mouthpiece), and those whose cheek pieces, being attached in a semisolid fashion, only move from left to right. Each cheek-piece design serves a specific purpose.

In the semisolid family, the cheek piece of many snaffle bits has a straight side. The full-cheek snaffle comes with a spoon above and below the mouthpiece. The half-cheek snaffle has a spoon either above or below the mouthpiece. The cheek pieces of the D-ring snaffle and the Don Dodge snaffle also meet the mouthpiece at a ninety-degree angle. These straight cheek pieces

serve two important purposes: they keep the bit from sliding through the horse's mouth, thereby injuring this sensitive area, and they add pressure on the side of the horse's mouth as you effect an opening rein. This added pressure point makes it even easier for the horse to recognize your aids. For instance, as you effect an opening rein to the left, the mouthpiece puts pressure on the left corner of the horse's lips and on his tongue; the straight side of the right cheek piece puts pressure on the right side of the horse's mouth as the bit slides very slightly to the left.

Another bit in the semisolid family of snaffles is the eggbutt, which has its origin in the hunt fields of England. The eggbut is popular with riders of large horses whose mouths can accommodate its large mouthpiece.

Loose-ring snaffles are well adapted to riding on loose reins. Because of its loose fitting in the end of the mouthpiece, the cheek piece vibrates and slides through the mouthpiece, sending subtle vibrations to the horse's mouth as you slowly take up the slack in the reins. These

vibrations cue your horse in advance to the aids you are about to apply and build a more sensitive and responsive performer. Rings come in different sizes and weights. The larger or heavier the ring, the more noticeable the rotating action is to the horse. Naturally, if you pick up quickly on the reins, you surprise your horse and cheat him out of this terrific learning aid.

Gag bits, also part of the loose-ring family of cheek pieces, apply pressure not only to the regular pressure points of the tongue and corners of the mouth, but also to the poll. They feature cheek-piece arrangements which guarantee 180-degree sliding action in the mouthpiece every time you make contact with the mouth. During the first 90 degrees of the rotation, the cheek piece simply slides through the mouthpiece, sending subtle vibrations to the horse's mouth. If your horse does not respond and you keep taking contact, the cheek piece draws the mouthpiece upward in the horse's mouth and the pressure on the poll increases. The amount of upward movement of the mouthpiece depends upon the position of your hands, the amount of contact, and the size of the rings. Rings of two to three inches in diameter usually slide the mouthpiece one inch up the mouth. Higher hands and strong contact increase the upward movement of the mouthpiece. As you keep taking the reins, the mouthpiece slides around the cheek piece until it stops against the upper port of the ring. At this point, the gag acts just like an eggbutt or D-ring snaffle. Since the headstall is essentially an extension of the reins, contact on the mouth also means pressure on the poll. This combination of downward poll pressure and upward bit movement makes the gag bit suitable for the most experienced hands only.

To be effective the gag must be adjusted correctly. While on loose reins, the mouthpiece and the rein stoppers should rest against the bottom parts of the rings. The mouthpiece should hang down in the interdental space of the horse's mouth with definitely no wrinkles at the corner of the lips. This position allows plenty of space for the mouthpiece to move without making contact with the pre-molars, contact that would hurt and frighten the horse.

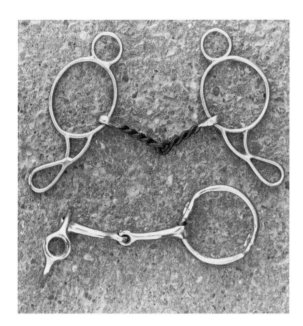

Gag bits. Above, gag bit designed to work on a regular headstall and reins. Below, gag bit with sliding rein ports through which the specially designed reins slide and apply poll and mouth pressure. (The left cheek piece was placed on its edge to show the sliding rein ports.) (Photo: Ted Gard)

All other factors being equal, bits of the semi-solid family of snaffles allow a horse to lay on the bit more comfortably than those of the loose-ring family; hence their use with young horses in whom we seek to build confidence in the bit, and with race horses who balance themselves on the bit for racing.

Except when riding with a full-cheek bit, all snaffle bit bridles should be mounted with a chinstrap to prevent the bit from sliding through the horse's mouth.

MOUTHPIECES

Three factors define the action of the snaffle's mouthpiece: its thickness, weight, and shape. The thicker mouthpiece is the mildest since it provides for a given amount of pressure to be applied over a larger surface of the horse's mouth. There is a limit, however, to how large a mouthpiece can be used. In most cases there is little room for a bit in a horse's mouth. The tongue fills the entire oral cavity. Therefore, a

thick mouthpiece used on a small-mouthed horse will cause excruciating pain as the joint hits the hard palate.

Mouthpieces vary in size from wire thin to almost one inch in diameter. If not used very carefully, the thin wire mouthpieces can be painful and even cause injury to the horse's mouth. Particularly severe and not necessary are

Various snaffle mouthpieces. Beginning at the top: very thin twisted wire, 3/8-inch smooth, Dr. Bristol, 3/8-inch smooth rollers, thick twisted wire, double-twisted wire, and rubber coated. (Photo: Ted Gard)

the double-twisted wire mouthpieces. Most breed associations and horse show organizations do not allow a horse to be shown in a mouthpiece that is less than 3/8-inch in diameter. With most stock-horse-type mounts, the largest mouthpiece you can use without causing discomfort to the horse is 3/8-inch in diameter.

The width of the mouthpiece is another factor. The mouthpiece should fit in the horse's mouth without any part of it showing on either side, and with the cheek pieces loosely touching but not pressing against the sides of the mouth. While most horses can be accommodated by the 5-inch-wide mouthpiece, smaller horses may need one between 4 and 4 1/2 inches wide. A mouthpiece that is too wide does not fit correctly over the tongue and bars and may cause injury inside the mouth. A too-narrow mouthpiece causes injury by pinching the lips between the cheek pieces and driving the cheek pieces into the side of the horse's face.

Excessive weight in the mouthpiece will fatigue the horse and desensitize his mouth as he seeks to carry and balance the bit. Larger-diameter mouthpieces, such as those over 5/8-inch, should be hollow to maintain a comfortable weight.

The shape of the mouthpiece in the snaffle bit varies greatly: it can have one or several joints, a solid bar, a large twist with sharp edges, a very fine twist, a square stock, or a smooth round stock. Mouthpieces may be wrapped with smooth wire or rubber, covered across their entire width with smooth rollers, or have frothers (small rings or beads) dangling from the middle.

The most common of all, however, is the smooth, single-jointed mouthpiece. With a diameter of a least 3/8-inch, it is the mildest of all mouthpieces and the most suited to schooling young horses. It is also the bit most recommended for use by beginner and intermediate riders.

Other shapes of single-jointed mouthpieces range from the relatively severe to the very severe, which include the entire selection of twisted-wire, thin-wire, wire-wrapped, and triangular mouthpieces. Although suitable for special purposes, such as lightening up the heavy-mouthed horse and retraining problem horses, these bits are best left to experienced, knowledgeable riders. Even in such competent hands, these bits should be used, at most, for three or four consecutive rides, after which the rider should go back to the regular-size mouthpieces. Used in this fashion, retraining bits move the horse along the reschooling path without building dependence on the correction mouthpiece. Many horses have been ruined by the abusive use (intentional or not) of twisted-wire and knife-edge (triangular) mouthpieces.

Double-jointed mouthpieces are capable of applying pressure to the bars of the mouth when the horse carries his head close to the vertical. This is made possible by the short center piece, which allows the remainder of the mouthpiece to bend around the tongue. For this reason, the double-jointed snaffle brings a lighter response from the horse, particularly one who tends to lean on the regular single-jointed mouthpiece.

The middle section of a double-jointed mouthpiece may take different forms. The most popular, the Dr. Bristol, features a small ring as the joint and, more often than not, smaller rings or beads of copper dangling from the center ring. These frothers induce salivation as the horse moves them with his tongue. The French Link is another version of the double-jointed mouthpiece. Its center piece is a simple round bar of small diameter, often covered by a copper roller. Yet another model of center piece is curved, somewhat like the low part on a curb bit, which provides room for the tongue and slightly more pressure on the bars.

A horse's mouth is more responsive when it is moist, when its salivary glands are activated. Since copper has been found to activate the salivary glands, it is an integral part of most mouthpieces. Copper is often used in the form of rollers over the mouthpiece, as a ring forming the joint, as frothers in the center of the mouthpiece, or simply inlaid in the bar stock itself.

The headstall should be adjusted so that the snaffle bit touches the corner of the horse's mouth but causes no wrinkles. This adjustment lets the horse carry the bit on his tongue. As a result, the bit applies pressure to a wider area of

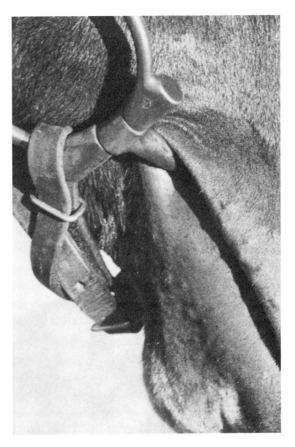

Correctly adjusted snaffle bit. The mouthpiece touches the corners of the lips without causing wrinkles. The cheek pieces are next to the horse's mouth but do not press into his face.

This snaffle bit is adjusted too tight. Notice how the mouthpiece causes the horse to "smile," as evidenced by the wrinkles at the corners of his lips. (Photo: Ted Gard)

the horse's mouth, which makes him more responsive. When you hold your hands low, the bit works on the tongue and the bars. When you hold your hands higher, more pressure is applied to the corners of the mouth. A bit that is adjusted too low in the horse's mouth or is too wide in the mouthpiece may possibly hit the horse's canines or incisors. Such low position encourages the horse to play with the bit or slip his tongue over it.

Of all the bits, the snaffle is the most versatile. It is the one used to start the colt and to school him through the intermediate level of training. Careful fitting of the snaffle bit to the horse, combined with attentive use of the aids, make it a most suitable tool for all types of riding and by all levels of riders.

CHAPTER 11

Curb Bits

The well-adjusted curb bit is designed for maximum lightness.

A curb bit is any bit, regardless of the type of mouthpiece, that works as a fulcrum and offers the rider leverage on the horse's mouth. The reins tie below the rings of the mouthpiece, to the lower end of elongated cheek pieces, called shanks. Curb bits may act on the tongue, bars, chin groove, poll, and possibly the roof of the mouth, or on a combination of those points, depending on the configuration of the mouthpiece.

In order to understand how the curb bit works, let's review what happens when you pick up on the reins. As you lift the slack from the reins and establish contact with the horse's mouth, the bottoms of the shanks tilt backward while the upper parts, above the mouthpiece, tilt forward. As the shanks move, the mouthpiece rotates in the horse's mouth. This is the first clue to the horse that you are asking for a maneuver. With the exception of mouthpieces angled to the front of the shanks, all curb bit mouthpieces rest on the horse's tongue. Hence, your horse feels this rotation through his tongue before pressure is applied to any other part of his mouth. As you keep taking up slack on the reins, the upper parts of the shanks pull the curb chain closer to the horse's chin groove. Until the curb chain touches the horse's chin you have merely taken slack out of the reins; the only signal to the horse of your new intentions being the subtle rotation of the mouthpiece in his mouth . Contact with the horse's mouth is established when the curb chain touches the chin. Continued take-up on the reins causes the curb chain to begin to clamp around the chin, forcing a rearward action of the mouthpiece, which in turn puts pressure on the designated parts of the horse's mouth: the tongue, the bars, the corners of the mouth, and the palate (if the

119

mouthpiece is so designed). The forward movement of the shanks causes a tightening of the headstall and consequently light pressure on the poll.

SHANKS

The shanks offer leverage through the counterpressure applied by the curb chain to the chin groove. You can affect the timeliness of the leverage by varying the adjustment of the curb chain. The amount of leverage you can exert depends, however, upon the ratio between that part of the shank measured from immediately above the mouthpiece to the top of the curb chain attachment and that part of the shank measured from immediately below the mouthpiece to the middle of the rein rings. A bit measuring $2\frac{1}{2}$ inches from the top of the mouthpiece to the top of the curb chain attachment and 5 inches from the mouthpiece to the middle of the reins has a ratio of 2 to 1. It is a milder bit, all other factors being equal, than one having a $1\frac{1}{2}$-inch cheek piece and a 7-inch shank below the mouthpiece, which has a ratio of 4.6 to 1.

All bits should be at least $1\frac{1}{2}$ inches long, from the top of the mouthpiece to the curb chain attachments. If the cheek piece is any shorter, there is a risk of pinching the corners of the horse's mouth between the mouthpiece and the curb strap as the bit rotates. A longer cheek piece increases the distance between the mouthpiece and the curb chain, thereby eliminating the risk of pinching. It also allows more rotation of the bit in the horse's mouth before the chin strap clamps on the jaw. This rotation is very important because it is the first cue to the horse of what the rider has in mind. Slow and gentle hands, reinforced with strong and timely leg and seat aids, will seldom need more than this rotation to guide a horse through a series of precise, electrifying maneuvers.

Shanks attach to the mouthpiece in two ways: the solid shank is welded solid to the mouthpiece, the loose jaw shank can rotate in the end of the mouthpiece. The loose jaw shank moves

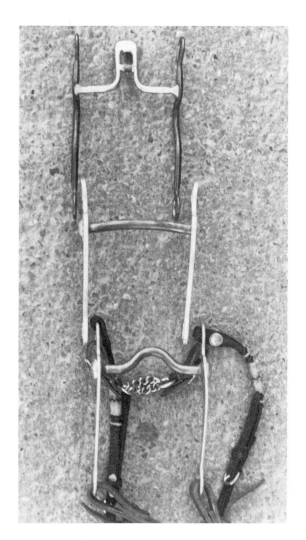

Curb bits with shanks of approximately the same overall length but with very different ratios. The bit at the top features a longer distance from the mouthpiece to the curb chain attachment than the other two bits. It has a ratio of 1 to 3. The center bit has a ratio of 1 to 5, whereas the bottom bit has a ratio of 1 to 7. Also interesting are the mouthpieces in these bits. From top to bottom, the Las Cruces, the mullen, and the medium port. (Photo: Ted Gard)

in the mouthpiece before contact is established, giving the horse advance notice of your aids. Through this preliminary action, the loose jaw shank gives the horse an earlier, gentler cue than the solid shank and contributes to turning out a lighter, more relaxed horse. In the case of the solid shank, all the softness must come from your aids and anything other than a very slow hand will certainly surprise your horse. As the loose shank swivels, it serves notice. The pressure is further diluted. It is gradual, predictable.

While the loose jaw shank attachment is suitable for direct and slightly open rein effects, the solid jaw bit should never be used with hands any wider than the distance between the shanks. Effect an opening rein with the solid shank bit and you pull the bit against the top of the horse's mouth on one side and against his molars on the opposite side.

Shanks come in a wide variety of shapes. Many of the variations in shape are purely aesthetic, but the amount of curvature in the shank is what is important. To evaluate the amount of curvature in a shank, draw a straight line from the curb chain ring past the near side of the mouthpiece and all the way down below the rein rings. The farther the rein rings fall behind the imaginary straight line, the greater the curvature in the shank. Some bits may have as much as three inches between the imaginary line and the rein rings. In others cases, the rein rings are placed directly in line with the mouthpiece and the curb chain attachment.

The greater the curvature in a shank, the milder the bit (all other factors being equal), as it gives the horse more of a signal before the lever effect comes into action. Bits built so that the rein rings hang directly below the horse's lips have more available rotation. Hence, they offer more range of leverage and are potentially more severe than bits with shanks that sweep back toward the horse. This is true to the point that if a curb bit had too much curvature in the shanks, its leverage effect would be eliminated. It would simply act as a snaffle, the shanks being an extension of the reins.

Bits featuring a pronounced curvature in the shanks are called overbalanced bits. The bottom part of the shanks of an overbalanced bit swing forward when you release the contact and feed slack to the reins, releasing the pressure on the curb chain and allowing the horse to carry his head in a natural position without pressure on the mouth or chin. These bits are ideal for events such as reining, cutting, or ranch work, and all other activities in which the horse carries his head naturally and on loose reins. Bits whose rein rings are close to, or in line with, the imaginary straight line are called underbalanced bits. They offer release from the pressure of the mouthpiece

The Buster Welch shank. This is an overbalanced bit. Notice the distance between the rein rings and the straight line drawn from the curb chain attachment and the rear of the mouthpiece. (Photo: Ted Gard)

and curb chain only when the horse carries his head in line with the bit's point of balance. Such bits are suited for events such as western pleasure and western riding, in which the horse is expected to carry his head in a collected position.

Straight-shank underbalanced bits often have an S-shaped lower shank to prevent the horse from mouthing the shank. Other features of shanks often play a role in the balancing of the bit. For example, the more metal there is behind the imaginary straight line running from the curb chain attachment past the mouthpiece and the entire length of the shanks, the more overbalanced the bit is likely to be. Hence, decoration on a bit almost always affects the way the bit works on the horse's mouth.

Some shanks offer a rein slot immediately behind the mouthpiece. This opening makes it possible to ride the horse with four reins, using the snaffle reins for new maneuvers and the curb reins for such things as neck reining or other exercises the horse performs well.

The rein rings are very close to the imaginary line from the curb chain attachment and rear of the mouthpiece. Consequently, this bit is underbalanced. Effectively, this bit will tend to hang straight down in the horse's mouth, putting pressure on his mouth and chin whenever he carries his head ahead of the vertical, even on loose reins. (Photo: Ted Gard)

MOUTHPIECES

In a study he conducted with the assistance of Texas A & M University, bit maker Greg Darnall concluded that the most sensitive part of the horse's mouth is the palate, followed by the tongue, then the bars, and finally the chin groove. With this in mind, let's look at various curb bit mouthpieces and how they communicate the movements of your hands.

The shape and size of the mouthpiece determines the pressure points affected by a bit. Just as with the snaffle bit, a thinner mouthpiece is more severe than a thicker one. Very thin wire mouthpieces, or chain mouthpieces, combined with the leverage afforded by the shanks, are very severe indeed. Many of these thin mouthpieces apply pressure to the bars and the tongue and are often fitted with a narrow curb chain. Such harsh combinations are not necessary if you take the time to learn how to use your aids correctly and school your horse at a pace suitable to him. In many instances, this sort of equipment is used by riders who try to make a horse do something he is neither prepared for nor has the ability to do. Developing your horsemanship skills and recognizing both your limitations and those of your horse go a long way toward avoiding abuse through the bit.

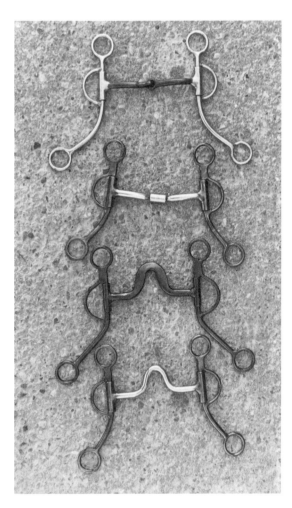

Various mouthpieces. From the top: regular jointed, Billy Allen, high port, medium port. (Photo: Ted Gard)

Curb bit mouthpieces come in various forms, one of the most popular of which is the jointed mouthpiece. The jointed mouthpiece offers the possibility of working one side of the horse's mouth independently from the other side. Because of this particularity, curb bits with this type of mouthpiece are very much like a snaffle and are well suited to basic schooling in the curb bit, including lateral bending and suppling exercises.

Jointed mouthpieces come in many shapes, including the simple center joint, the "life saver" ring (with or without frothers), the Billy Allen, and the double-jointed correction bit. With the exception of the Billy Allen, all of the jointed mouthpieces apply pressure to the tongue and have the potential of pressure to the bars. Because its joint is encased in a sleeve, the Billy Allen mouthpiece bends very little. Therefore, the mouthpiece cannot press on the bars but rather rests on the tongue.

Of the solid mouthpieces, the mullen is recommended for horses who have a thicker tongue than average and therefore little space between the tongue and the palate. Mullen mouthpieces are to be used by experienced and careful hands only. Many horses have suffered tongue damage from the hands of temperamental or uneducated riders jerking the slack out of the reins of a mullen mouthpiece.

The sweetwater mouthpiece is designed to be used on horses who have suffered tongue damage or who do not respond well to tongue pressure. Upon contact, the mouthpiece presses on the bars while the wide port leaves plenty of room for the tongue.

The low- and medium-port mouthpieces utilize tongue pressure when the rider makes light contact. Apply stronger contact and, its port being too low for the entire tongue to fit in, the mouthpiece engages the bars as well as the tongue.

The high-port bit allows enough room for the tongue to fit into the port, hence the absence of tongue pressure. As your contact rotates the bit in the horse's mouth, the bottom corners of the port come down on each side of the tongue and press on the bars. Any port whose length from the bottom of the mouthpiece to the top of the port is at least two inches is considered a high port. Such a port may or may not apply palate pressure, depending on the size of the horse's mouth and the adjustment of the curb chain. A loose curb chain allows more rotation of the mouthpiece and a greater potential for palate pressure. High-port mouthpieces include the U.S., the Salinas, the cathedral, the Las Cruces, and all spade bits. Some spade bits have a roller in the bottom of the port, however, and therefore do not offer tongue release.

To offer any palate pressure, a mouthpiece must have a port or spoon measuring more than two inches from the bottom of the mouthpiece stock to the top of the port. Palate pressure ports with a sharp edge at the top are considered very severe, since the contact with the palate is concentrated in a very small area. More acceptable are the spoon ports, whose rounded surface greatly reduces the risk of injury to the horse's mouth. Also important to the degree of severity of the port is its angle in relation to the balance of the bit. Let the bit balance itself on your fingers, and notice whether the port is on the same axis as the cheek pieces. A port positioned on the same axis as the cheek pieces engages the palate as soon as the bit begins to rotate. A port whose top spoon section is located behind the axis allows rotation of the mouthpiece, which gives notice to the horse before pressure is felt on the palate. Bits designed to apply palate pressure should be used by very experienced hands only.

CURB CHAINS AND STRAPS

The curb chain (or strap) is an essential element on the curb bit. Without it the curb bit loses its leverage action and becomes a very ineffective, misfitted, and even hurtful device.

Not only is the curb strap essential, but its adjustment is critical. The curb chain should rest on the horse's jaw, just above the fleshy part of the chin. Adjust it so as to permit some rotation of the mouthpiece in the horse's mouth before the curb chain applies pressure to the chin. Do not make it so loose, however, that

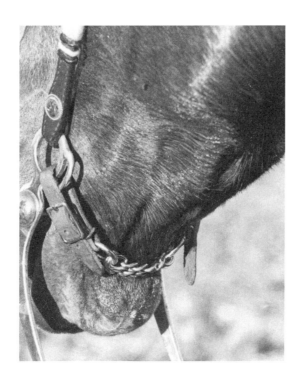

This curb chain allows some movement of the shanks before pressing on the horse's jaw and causing a leverage effect on the mouth. (Photo: Ted Gard)

the forward movement of the cheek pieces draws the curb strap close to the corners of the mouth and pinches the lips against the mouthpiece. Too loose, the curb strap destroys the purpose of the curb: leverage is practically nonexistent. Then when you take up on the reins, the mouthpiece is pulled up in the horse's mouth, hitting the molars and causing pain and resistance to the aids. Too tight, and you surprise your horse whenever you take up on the reins by not allowing enough rotation of

the mouthpiece before the curb chain clamps on the horse's chin.

You may choose between curb chains and curb straps, which have many variations within each family. Chains are totally acceptable and safe when they are fitted and used correctly. If you choose to use a curb chain, it should be a minimum of one-half inch wide and lay flat against the horse's chin. Twisted or narrow chains cause injury to the chin and eventually cause the horse to develop scar tissue and even calcification of the mandible (lower jaw). Such harsh tools are signs of riders who are not willing to take the time to school their horses or to develop the skills necessary for correct horsemanship.

Should you choose to use a strap, select a type that will not stretch, such as one made of braided cord or heavier leather. Stretchy chin straps let the horse evade your aids because he is comfortable pushing against the contact.

Many riders are afraid of hurting their horse with a curb chain and would rather use a strap. These riders should realize that unless they use their hands well, they will cause awful damage and pain in the horse's mouth regardless of whether they use a strap or chain.

The well-adjusted curb bit is designed for maximum lightness: the slower a rider picks up on the reins, the more notice the horse gets; the lighter and more subtle the cue, the softer the performance.

CHAPTER 12

Bitting Devices

Bitting devices will never replace your ability to apply your aids effectively.

Over centuries of schooling horses, riders have developed a number of tools to assist in the bitting and training of their horses. In the hands of educated, well-seated riders, these tools are often effective. Used by abusive or inexperienced hands they lead to more problems than they can solve. In this chapter, I describe the construction and function of the most popular and most misunderstood bitting devices and discuss the purpose and correct adjustment of each. In addition, I detail the principles of their use and explain the problems you will bring upon yourself and your horse if you do not adhere to these principles.

DRAW REINS

Popular among bitting devices, draw reins are designed to help in schooling a horse to accept and give to the bit. Their use should result in a horse becoming equally supple to the left and to the right and responding readily to subtle leg, seat, and hand aids. He should flex at the poll and never push against the bit, maintaining a soft feel regardless of the maneuver performed.

Draw reins are usually about ten feet long and made of leather, nylon, or simple ³/₈-inch or ¹/₂-inch rope. They attach to either the cinch between the horse's front legs or to the cinch D rings on each side of the horse. The reins then run through the snaffle bit cheek pieces and to the rider's hands.

Shorten, lengthen, or even release draw reins, depending upon the exercise performed and the needs of the horse you are riding. In the case of this horse, he needs slightly more support from the draw reins for a particular exercise, therefore the rider shortened the draw reins so the horse may feel their action more than that of the regular reins. After completion of the exercise, she will lengthen the draw reins and use regular reins.

When attached to the cinch between the horse's front legs, draw reins bring the horse not only to flex at the poll but also to lower his entire neck, from the withers to the poll. This setting is often preferred by trainers of western pleasure and equitation horses. Because the attachment of the cinch D rings is higher, the horse flexes at the poll as a result of giving but does not need to lower his neck as much to give to the pressure. This arrangement is preferred by those schooling horses for reining, barrel racing, and ranch work, since during these activities it is desirable for the horse to maintain a higher head and neck.

Draw reins should be used with snaffle bits only—never with curb bits—for three reasons. First, a horse that needs draw reins has not learned to accept the bit and respond to contact by relaxing and giving. Therefore, he is not ready for a curb bit and should not be ridden with one. Second, the combination of downward and rearward pull exerted by the draw reins is somewhat the opposite of the slightly upward pressure applied by the curb bit. Third, and most compelling: the power afforded your hands by the draw reins, when combined with that of a curb bit, may cause a horse to resist more than ever before, even to the point of rearing up.

Correct attachment and choice of bit is not all there is to using draw reins effectively. Applying them to the right type of horse is of key importance. Since they work as a type of pulley, draw reins increase the power in your hands, which is why they are particularly helpful in retraining stiff horses who have a great deal of natural impulsion and plenty of schooling, but who need gentle convincing that they cannot avoid using their body correctly in response to your aids.

Because of the power they afford your hands, draw reins should not be used on green colts or very nervous horses. Such horses usually overreact to the intimidating contact and begin to seek ways to escape it, often overflexing or rearing up. Draw reins should not be used on naturally lethargic horses. What little natural impulsion they have is often stifled by the strong bit contact. Before he faces draw reins, your horse should already understand how to respond to bit pressure.

Correct use of draw reins depends on the effective coordination of your seat, leg, and hand aids. And before you ride with draw reins, you must know how and have sufficient feel to ride a horse forward and in balance (see chapter 13; for coordinating your aids to achieve it, see chapters 14 and 15.)

If you use draw reins correctly, you should feel considerable change in your horse's responsiveness within two or three schooling sessions. Improvement will continue, but in smaller daily increments. Avoid using draw reins for more than five or six continuous schooling sessions. If your horse shows no changes by then, you are not using your aids correctly; further use of the draw reins will lead only to enhanced problems with your horse. If you do see his performance improve, give yourself and your horse a chance to build on these improvements by riding with regular reins only, trying to achieve the same results you were getting with the draw reins. If the draw reins are still needed, use them again, but avoid using them continuously. Otherwise, you will create a dependency on them. Your goal is to eliminate the need for draw reins through improved suppleness and responsiveness in your horse.

THE GERMAN MARTINGALE

The German martingale is a combination regular rein and draw rein. It serves the same purpose as the draw reins/regular reins held together. The advantage of the German martingale is that you need hold only one rein in each hand rather than two reins, as with the draw reins. Therefore, if your horse is at a stage when changing the adjustment of the draw rein as you ride is not critical, the German martingale can simplify your task.

German martingales can be made of leather, leather and cord, or braided cord. They have regular reins that attach to the snaffle's cheek pieces. These regular reins are mounted with a form of anchoring device (D ring, buckle, etc.) about sixteen to eighteen inches behind the snaffle attachment. A draw rein, which attaches to the regular rein's anchoring device, runs through the snaffle's cheek piece and attaches either at the cinch D ring or between the horse's legs.

Adjustment of the German martingale depends on the effect desired on the horse. Let's assume that your horse roots his nose forward when you make contact with his mouth. Adjust the martingale so that contact on the bit comes from the regular reins without engaging the draw reins, and so that the draw reins, although not active, are tight when contact is established. In this way, the draw reins will come into play and apply downward pressure on the horse's mouth as soon as he roots his nose forward. With this adjustment, your horse learns to travel with a natural head and neck position and not to push against your hands when you make contact. However, since the draw reins do not activate unless the horse pushes his nose forward, your horse does not learn to give at the poll.

Should you wish to use the German martingale to teach a difficult horse to give at the poll, you need the draw rein to activate as you make contact with the horse's mouth. In this case, shorten the draw rein so that the horse feels the effect of the draw rein before the

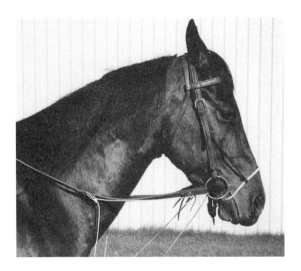

This German martingale is adjusted so the regular reins engage the bit and the draw reins are acti-vated only if the horse raises his head or pushes against the bit.

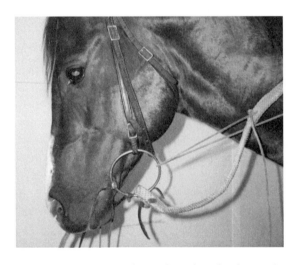

This German martingale is adjusted so the draw rein action engages the bit before the regular rein (note the loose regular rein). Once the regular rein is fully extend-ed, then it takes over the contact and the draw rein becomes loose, having served its purpose.

regular rein tightens on the bit. As you keep taking up on the reins, the regular rein eventually straightens and engages the bit. When this happens, the draw reins slacken and their effect is eliminated. The horse feels regular contact.

The horse does not get relief from the draw rein until the regular rein takes over and engages the bit. Therefore, adjust the draw reins so that the regular reins engage the bit at the point at which your horse's head is in the desired position. This may be at any point

This German martingale is adjusted so the regular reins are fully extended when the horse's head is perpendicular to the ground. With another one-half inch of flexion at the poll, the draw reins will become loose and the horse will be responding to regular reins only.

between the natural carriage and the vertical, but of course never behind the vertical.

With German martingales, as with draw reins, the danger exists that the horse may become dependent on the device, particularly with any adjustment during which the draw reins act before the regular reins. German martingales, like draw reins, should be used with caution and within a plan to wean the horse as soon as possible.

THE RUNNING MARTINGALE

The running martingale is another popular and effective bitting device. The running martingale, like draw reins and the German martingale, prevents your horse from raising his head and pushing his nose out, thereby evading the bit.

The popularity of the running martingale undoubtedly comes from the fact that it is relatively easy to use. Just adjust it, slide the reins through the free-moving rings, and ride without concern with double reins. As you make contact with the horse's mouth, the reins slide through the rings and unless the horse raises his head,

contact is similar to that of a regular snaffle bit. If your horse raises his head in response to the contact, the downward pressure applied by the rings on the reins forces the bit to engage the bars of his mouth as well as his tongue. Finding his resistance less comfortable than a simple response, the horse soon chooses the most comfortable path and learns to respond without raising his head.

Running martingales are made of leather, nylon, cord, or braided cord and come in various designs. All have a fork terminated by rings through which the reins run, as well as a single cinch strap that attaches to the cinch between your horse's front legs. The better-built running martingales incorporate a collar that goes around your horse's neck. If you ride your horse with a breast collar affixed to the cinch between your horse's front legs, the running martingale may be as simple as a fork that attaches to the center ring of the breast collar. Stay away from elastic running martingales. Their stretchy nature does not offer resistance to the escaping horse and only contributes to reaffirming the problems. A suitable running martingale has an adjustment buckle on each strap of the fork, cinch strap, and collar so that you can make the proper adjustment on any horse.

And correct adjustment is paramount to successful results. Too long, the martingale is unsafe and serves no purpose. Too short, it encourages your horse to fight the bit and find other ways of resisting contact, such as

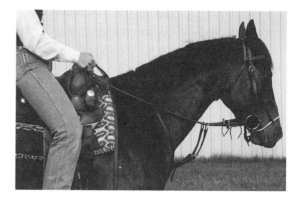

Correctly adjusted running martingale. The rein ring intersects a straight line from the rider's hand to the horse's mouth when his head is in a natural position.

overflexing or lowering the entire neck below the withers. Place the collar around your horse's neck, just in front of the withers. Set the buckle so that the main ring, which unites all the straps, is located at the base of his neck. Too low and the forks may not be long enough for the desired effect on your horse's mouth; too high and the ring will injure the base of his neck. Snap the cinch strap to the cinch between the horse's front legs and adjust it so that it is taut but not tight. Not only is a loose cinch strap an invitation for your horse to step into it, but it also may slide up when your horse pulls against the bit, thus destroying the effectiveness of the martingale. Adjust the fork straps so that the rings allow for a straight line in the reins from your hands to the horse's mouth when your horse holds his head in a natural position. Running martingales, like draw reins, are to be used with snaffle bits only.

Always use stoppers on your reins when you ride with a running martingale. These small rubber rectangles slide over the reins and are a very inexpensive key to preventing potentially fatal accidents. Riders and horses may be injured when a martingale ring is allowed to slide to the bit end of the rein and get lodged in the buckle or leather tie. With the rider unable to release the contact, the horse finds himself trapped and often reacts violently. Avoid using martingales that go from the cinch directly to the reins without any sort of chest attachment. They hang low between the horse's legs and are a potential hazard.

Like other bitting devices, the running martingale will not make up for a poor seat and incorrect application of the aids. When well-adjusted and used properly, however, it can help you and your horse to a higher level of horsemanship.

THE STANDING MARTINGALE

The standing martingale, also known as a tie-down, is another popular bitting device. Its purpose is to prevent your horse from raising his head too far up and back or from pushing his nose too far forward. It differs from other martingales in that it has no relationship to the reins or bit. This means that the tie-down does not lead your horse to respond to the bit in a different manner. In other words, with correct use of the other bitting devices, your horse eventually learns to change his response pattern. But even correct use of the tie-down will not change a horse's bad habit of raising his head in response to bit pressure. Although the tie-down prevents him from raising his head too high while he is wearing it, after you take it off your horse still has the problem behavior.

Nevertheless, the tie-down definitely has its place in performance horsemanship. It is particularly helpful on horses whose repeated high-speed performances lead to a very high level of anticipation. By their very nature, events such as barrel racing, roping, and pole bending build anticipation of a hard start from a virtual stand-still. Any horse anticipating having to give so much of himself in a matter of seconds will become anxious and begin to push against the bit, no matter how appropriate the aids used.

A standing martingale is composed of three main parts: the strap, the collar, and the noseband. The strap, which can be leather or nylon, attaches to the cinch by means of a snap and is affixed to the noseband. The collar is important because it prevents the strap from hanging low between the horse's legs and causing potentially fatal accidents. The noseband, which goes around the horse's head, can be made of rope, leather, nylon, or steel cable.

Again, adjustment of the standing martingale is key to its usefulness and important to the safety of you and your horse. The collar should be adjusted so that the strap follows the contours of your horse's neck. This is paramount, for a low-hanging strap is an invitation to your horse to step into it, thereby causing a potentially fatal accident.

Adjust the cinch strap so that it follows the line of the lower jaw and the neck when lifted to the the level of the lower jaw. Longer than this, the standing martingale is not effective. Shorter than this, it hinders your horse's ability to use his head and neck as a balancing pendulum. The result could be a disastrous performance. Unable to balance himself properly, your horse might not stop as hard as he could at that calf, or he might not be able to run and turn the barrel as fast as he could if the tie-down were of the correct length.

Choose a flat noseband. If it is rope, it should be covered with leather and at least 1/2 inch in diameter. Avoid wire nosebands. Even when covered with leather, they are too harsh and may cause injury to your horse. Besides, it is not necessary to inflict pain on the horse to keep him from raising his head. Adjust the head piece so that the noseband rests just below the bony protrusions on the side of your horse's head. Any lower and the pressure your horse puts on himself as he tries to raise his head may damage the cartilage in the lower part of the bridge of his nose.

Since they have no interaction with the bit and reins, standing martingales can be used with any type of bit.

Do not use ear tie-downs (ties with a loop over the poll). They are not necessary and often cause injury to horses. Finally, do not use a standing martingale to change your horse's behavior or punish him for raising his head. This approach often leads riders to set the cinch strap too short, causing the horse to fight the restrictive setting even to the point of rearing up.

The standing martingale is a useful tool for some horses and riders. Use it properly and enjoy an enhanced horsemanship experience. Use it incorrectly and put both you and your horse in danger of a crippling accident.

The Cavesson

The cavesson, also known as a noseband or mouth shutter, is a simple piece of equipment used to keep a horse from opening his mouth to escape the pressure of the bit. Although some are made of leather, most are made of rope with a light cord crown piece.

Cavessons can be placed above the bit or below the bit. Both settings work well on most horses.

A cavesson placed below the bit is called a dropped noseband. The dropped noseband is slightly more effective because its position is such that when your horse opens his mouth, pressure is applied to the sensitive cartilage on the top of his nose. Be sure the noseband is set immediately below the bit and at an upward angle in the front, to keep the horse's nostrils amply free for breathing during workout. Too many riders forget this important detail and deprive their horses of a necessary supply of air during heavy workouts. The result is muscle soreness and limited schooling.

Should you choose a cavesson fitted above the bit, take care that it is fitted correctly. It should be far enough above the bit to avoid pinching the corners of the horse's mouth between the cavesson and the bit.

Most horses should be ridden with a cavesson most of the time, particularly those who tend to resist the hands and those who open their mouths when asked to perform any exercise.

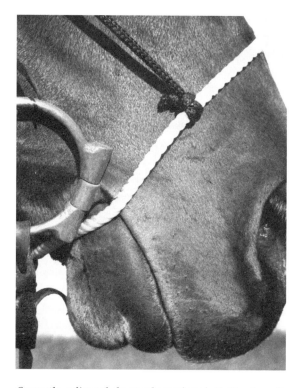

Correctly adjusted dropped noseband. Notice how it bends around the mouthpiece in order to fit in the chin groove yet it is sufficiently high on the nose to allow for expansion of the nostrils.

Be careful when fitting a cavesson on a horse who has not worn one before. Many horses have an unpleasant reaction if they are in the habit of opening their mouths but are suddenly restricted by a cavesson. Reaction can vary from tossing the head in an attempt to evade the cavesson, to rearing. Therefore, if your horse has the habit of opening his mouth, take extra precautions if you decide to put a cavesson on him. Be sure to lunge the horse with the bit and cavesson, giving him the opportunity to get accustomed to it before you get on his back.

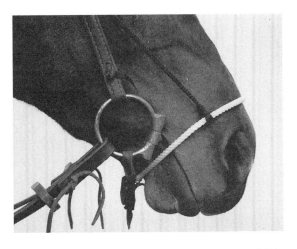

Because this dropped cavesson is too low, it inhibits expansion of the nostrils and restricts breathing during workout.

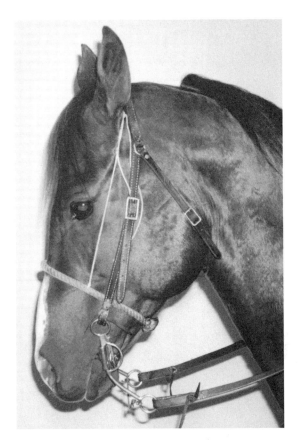

Correctly adjusted cavesson. It is fitted high enough on the horse's nose to prevent the mouthpiece from pinching the lips against it.

CHAPTER 13

Bitting

The way a horse responds to the bit is entirely man-made.

K nowing the mechanics of bits takes you only part way along the road to successful horsemanship. To complete the journey, you also need to understand how the different responses horses have to bits affect their performance under saddle. And you need to understand and be able to apply key principles of the usage of bits. In this chapter I detail how horses respond to bit pressure and I will discuss the advantages and disadvantages of each way. Then I outline key principles of the use of bits. I conclude the chapter with helpful advice on the progression of bits from snaffles to curbs. But first, the ways by which horses respond to contact.

The way a horse reacts to the bit will dramatically affect his whole performance, which is why it is very important that you understand the four basic ways horses respond to bitting: above the bit, behind the bit, accepting the bit, and on the bit. Regardless of the training your horse has had, or the type of riding that has been done with him so far, he responds to bit pressure in either one or a combination of these four patterns. Above and behind the bit offer no benefits to riding performance. Accepting the bit is a sufficient level of response for horses used in trail riding, although riders might find horses with more schooling more interesting. For any type of more sophisticated riding, such as horse show events, your horse should readily respond to your aids by going on the bit.

ABOVE THE BIT

A horse is said to be above the bit when his head is carried unnaturally high. This horse resist your hands by thrusting his nose forward and his head upward.

Travelling above the bit is somewhat normal with very green horses. They are weak in the back and are uncomfortable carrying their rider's weight. Their understanding of how to use their muscles to respond to bit pressure is very limited. In these cases it is not a fault but a temporary reaction, soon to be eliminated through strength building and schooling exercises (see chapter 14, Body Control).

Roping horses, barrel racing horses, and other gymkhana horses are often above the bit in anticipation of a race. To an extent, this is due to the excitement of the event. There are no stimuli the trainer can use to get the horse on the bit at this point. Still, the winningest of horses soon lowers his head and accepts the bit as the race begins—he finds a way to relieve the tension by going through the moves of the regular training routines.

The horse who moves above the bit is "strung out." His back is hollow, his hindquarters are not engaged. The rider has very little control over the horse's shoulders and even less control over his torso and hindquarters. Consequently, the horse often picks up the wrong lead, turns considerably better on one side than the other, backs up crooked, stops crooked, and moves readily away from the leg pressure on one side but moves into the leg going the other way. The horse is stiff and unable to perform smoothly.

The spoiled horse who has been travelling above the bit, because of mistraining and rough, abusive hands, is very difficult to cure. When mounted on such a horse, be sure to use a smooth snaffle bit. Anything more severe will only confirm the horse's fears of the hands and bit. As the horse's head comes up and he comes above the bit, raise your hands as high as the horse's nose and hold until the horse, looking for relief and comfort, begins to lower his head. All the while the horse is above the bit, drive

This horse is above the bit. (Photo: Ted Gard)

him forward with strong impulsion legs. In doing this, you make the high head position so uncomfortable that the horse will try to escape the only way he can: by lowering the head.

But lowering the head becomes an escape only if you reward it. Therefore, you must release all pressures as soon as the horse *begins* to lower his head. The timing is critical if the horse is to associate the comfortable reward of release with the lowering of his head. It is of paramount importance that the rider holds rather than pulls with the hands (see chapter 9, The Hands).

BEHIND THE BIT

A horse who goes behind the bit shows his reluctance to accept pressure on his mouth. He evades the bit by overflexing his neck and tucking his chin in close to his chest. This fault seriously impairs the quality of movement because he is afraid to go forward. Since he will not let you elevate him with the bit, this horse is typically on his forehand, with a hollow back and his hindquarters strung out behind him. Riding with speed makes it difficult to control any part of his body; it is as if you were riding him with nothing on his head.

His head well behind the vertical, this horse is behind the bit. Horses behind the bit evade the contact and in doing so make it impossible for the rider to hold them in the bridle while driving their hindquarters under them for collection. (Photo: Ted Gard)

Horses are brought behind the bit by heavy, unyielding, and uneducated hands. Others have been taught to overflex by excessive use of draw reins, poorly adjusted running martingales, or bitting rigs of any sort. Yet other horses are behind the bit because the rider has tried to achieve flexion by pulling on the reins rather than using his legs to drive the horse forward.

Retraining the horse who moves behind the bit is a difficult task. The horse must learn to move forward and to know that the rider will not hurt him when he takes contact. This is best accomplished by using a smooth snaffle, very little hands and much impulsion in the legs to drive the horse forward at a fast trot and brisk walk. The horse will begin to lower his head and extend his neck. At this point, the rider must give the horse as much reins as possible while keeping them lightly stretched. In time, the horse will accept the bit.

ACCEPTING THE BIT

The horse accepts the bit when he willingly moves forward and without resistance while contact is applied to his mouth. He accepts rearward pressure from the bit without rooting his nose out, opening his mouth or getting above or behind the bit.

Acceptance of the bit is the foundation of putting the horse on the bit. It begins with lateral flexion and continues with longitudinal flexion (see the following discussion of being on the bit, as well as the discussion of aids in chapter 14). It terminates with true collection: putting the horse on the bit.

ON THE BIT

Your horse is said to be on the bit when he is balanced and carries himself in an engaged frame without seeking the support of the reins. He responds to your impulsion legs by moving forward and flexing at the poll. He is very responsive to your leg and seat aids and moves into lateral movements and transitions without ever bracing against your hands. His hindquarters are driven further underneath his body as his shoulders elevate and his back lifts up under the saddle. His body shortens as his center of gravity moves back. As he moves, his hind feet print the ground farther forward than they would if the horse were moving in a natural state.

It is not necessary to have contact on the horse's mouth at all times in order to have him on the bit. Ultimately, your horse becomes so light and responsive that the mere weight of the reins between the bit and your hand is sufficient contact to keep him on the bit at all times during performance. Consequently, a horse may be ridden on loose reins and still be on the bit. In fact, a horse is truly on the bit only when he has attained a level of self-carriage and can remain in a balanced frame even when ridden on loose reins.

This horse moves forward on the bit. His poll is elevated. His head is perpendicular to the ground. He reaches deep under himself with his hind legs, an indication that his back is round under the saddle and his center of gravity has shifted back. (Photo: Ted Gard)

Once your horse is fully on the bit, he has not only attained a higher level of responsiveness but he also displays another very important quality: softness. He performs all gaits, maneuvers, and transitions in a compliant manner.

To the performance horse, being able to go on the bit properly and quickly is very important. For when he is working through an event, the western horse must be able to change rapidly from an extended frame as he runs hard, to a fully engaged form for a sliding stop, a short turn around the barrel, or a fast back up. The paralyzing effect of resistance to the aids truly becomes clear when one adds speed to a maneuver.

A horse shows his resistance to the aids by stiffening his body. In practical terms, this means that the horse cannot perform various maneuvers at his best because his opposition to the aids restricts his range of motion. Hence the bouncing spins, the disunited lope, the wide turn around that first barrel, the bouncy stop, or the head raised high in the air during a transition. All of these problems and countless others can be solved by putting the horse on the bit.

PRINCIPLES OF USING BITS

In general, riders tend to use bits that are too sophisticated and severe for their level of expertise and the schooling their horses have received. Most riders would do well to use basic bits: a snaffle with a smooth mouthpiece for basic schooling, intermediate training, and trail riding; a loose-shank, jointed-mouthpiece curb bit for specialized training in western pleasure, trail, western riding, roping, and reining; a loose-jaw low- to high-port curb for finishing in the same events.

If a problem develops in the training of any horse, always go back to the milder bit. Years of experience in training riders and their horses have shown me that most training problems originate from a horse stiffening his jaw, his poll, his neck, his shoulders, his ribcage, and his hindquarters in anticipation of being hurt in the mouth. The mildest of bits and the softest of hands will build up the horse's confidence. He will begin to relax and give to pressure instead of bracing himself for pain.

Invariably, a horse begins to fear the bit, bracing against it when the rider, intentionally or not, pulls and jerks on the horse's mouth and causes pain. Therefore, until you have achieved an independent seat, you should limit the bits you use to the mildest of all, perhaps a smooth mouthpiece snaffle.

Never go from a mild bit to more severe bit with the idea of inflicting more pain on the horse to solve a performance problem. In most cases this solution is short-lived. You succeed in inflicting more pain on the horse for a day or two, get a more suitable response, then have to go back to the legal bit for showing and find that your horse does not respond as he did at home. Frightened, confused, unschooled mounts will not perform better in response to being hurt more. Rather, the pain only reinforces their fear and fuels their confusion. Little by little the horse becomes less responsive to the severe bit and the hunt is on for one even more severe. Performance problems are resolved by using a milder bit, more effective aids, and more schooling on the basics.

Also flawed is the approach in which the rider changes bits every second or third ride so that the horse cannot get used to a single bit. This shows an extremely shallow knowledge of horsemanship. No combination of bits can make up for such a rider's lack of effectiveness in the application of the aids.

The use of slow hands, from light, asking contact to increased pressure, holding, and yielding is described in chapter 9. Rereading that chapter now might be helpful, in light of what you now know about bits.

TRANSITION FROM SNAFFLES TO CURBS

Because of their effectiveness and simplicity of use compared to other equipment, snaffle bits are ideal for use on green horses or with green riders. However, the time comes in the schooling of the horse or in the development of the rider when changing from a snaffle bit to a curb bit is beneficial. Such a transition should not be made without thoughtful analysis of how the horse currently responds and what performance objectives you are striving to achieve. The following are guidelines for a smooth transition.

The first point to consider is whether you have enough balance and seat that at no time will the movements of the horse's back be communicated to his mouth through your hands. Bouncy hands are bad on the horse even with the mildest of snaffles. A curb bit's leverage will multiply the pulls and jerks, resulting in a very scared and stiff horse. It often takes years to develop the independent seat necessary to ride effectively with a curb bit and the effort is well worth the time involved. Great personal rewards await you when your skills reach that level of accomplishment. But do not rush things at the expense of your horse.

Another point to consider: does my horse need a curb bit? Many horses are never asked to perform at a high level of collection and intensity. For these horses, such as family horses and trail riding horses, a snaffle bit is not only the most comfortable to wear, but also the most bit they will ever need.

Finally, before you consider which bit should come after the snaffle, you must answer positively the question: Is my horse ready for the curb bit?

Your horse is ready for the curb bit if he goes on the bit readily in response to very light aids at all three gaits. He is ready for the curb bit if he guides on the circle, stops softly on his hocks without pushing against the bit, and flexes at the poll whenever you take the slack out of the reins. He is ready for the curb bit if you can perform haunches-in (move his hindquarters) at the walk, to the left and to the right, without any resistance on his part. Your horse is ready for the curb bit if he bends equally to the right and to the left while flexed at the poll and on light aids. All of these actions test a horse's suppleness and responsiveness. If your horse fails one of these tests he is not ready for the curb bit; moving him into one will lead to further resistance on his part. You must gain control of your horse's entire body with the mildest bit if you are to avoid problems later on.

If you are an experienced rider, it should take no more than four months from the time you first saddle a colt to the time he is ready for a curb bit. If it takes longer, don't despair. It is more important to do it right than to do it fast. Keep riding and focusing. Experience comes only through smart and hard work.

If your horse passes the tests, move him from the smooth mouthpiece Don Dodge or O-ring snaffle to a short-shank Billy Allen curb bit. This bit, such as the one made by bit maker Greg Darnall of Lone Oak, Texas, offers many advantages for the horse new to curb bits. Its low ratio of 1 to 2 gives it a mild leverage. Its loose jaw shanks give the horse time to feel a rein command before the mouthpiece begins to rotate. The jointed mouthpiece enables you to work on one side of the horse's mouth independently from the other—an important feature when you are moving from a snaffle that works one side at a time. The Billy Allen swivel joint, named after the trainer who designed it, keeps the mouthpiece from bending over on itself, thus reducing the pressure points to the tongue and chin only. Adjust the curb chain so that it is relatively loose for the first few rides.

Use your hands very slowly for the first few rides and work mostly on lateral bending, giving the horse plenty of time to get familiar with the curb action. Do not expect the same level of performance you were getting with the snaffle. Wait for the horse to give it to you in the new bit. Then continue to ride the horse the same way you ride him with the snaffle bit.

The Don Dodge ³/₈-inch smooth snaffle and the short-shank Billy Allen should take you and your horse past the intermediate level of training, regardless of the event you want to specialize in. Once your horse performs his

event close to perfection in the short-shank Billy Allen, you may want to move him into a long-shank Billy Allen or a short-shank, loose-jaw curb with a medium port. After the horse is completely schooled, you can use a solid-shank bit. Keep in mind, however, that sometimes you will likely need to go back to the loose shanks and jointed mouthpieces to keep him supple and correct.

Stay with the types of bits approved as legal by the breed or show association you plan to show with. Use your aids correctly and enjoy a horse who trusts you and performs out of training and not out of fear, responding lightly and on the bit.

The way a horse responds to the bit is entirely man-made. Understanding how that response affects the horse's performance, and respecting some important principles of bitting, including transitions from snaffles to curbs, opens a challenging future to you and your horse.

PART V

So far I have introduced you to safety around horses and guided you through some basic handling. Together we have worked on mental preparation for effective horsemanship, worked on your balance and seat, and discussed the correct body position at all gaits. I have explained the mechanics of posting and how to do it correctly. An in-depth study of the leg, seat, and hand aids revealed how to use your body for successful horsemanship. Finally, an all-encompassing section on bits and bitting prepared you for the rest of this book: how to put it all together for fun and challenge.

In this part of the book I explain how to coordinate all your aids for a winning performance in the most popular western events. I describe the component maneuvers and discuss the aids applicable for their correct execution in each event.

This part of the book does not list the procedures involved in schooling your horse. To do that would require a volume for each event. Nevertheless, once you have an understanding of the maneuver and a clear idea of the aids used in performing it, you can determine the best schooling approach for your horse.

Chapter 14 leads you through the exercises and aids useful in controlling your horse's body. Chapter 15 focuses on the challenging events of western pleasure and trail and chapter 16 slides you through the exciting sport of reining. Barrel racing and pole bending are blood-curdling events for which you will find help in chapter 17, along with information about the incredible sport of cutting. Learn how to sit a cutting horse through one of those explosive stops and turns in front of a determined cow.

CHAPTER 14

Body Control

"For any horse to perform correctly, the rider must be in control of the body parts."

—*Craig Johnson*

Body control is very important to your horse's performance. It serves to prepare him for the demanding maneuvers required in the show or rodeo arena. During this stage of riding, you put your horse through a series of progressive exercises that not only develop his responsiveness to your aids but also supple and strengthen his body. In turn, you gain complete control of every square inch of his body, enabling you to position your horse for maximum smoothness and speed of execution.

These exercises are not the only way to put you and your horse on the path to becoming a specialized and polished performance team but, once mastered, they do offer a solid foundation to come back to when the finished product begins to falter. In fact, successful performance-horse trainers spend a few minutes during every training session on all of these exercises. This review allows them to detect stiffness and resistance to the aids before it becomes engraved in the horse's mind. On a daily basis, they can analyze the cause of a budding problem and solve it before the finished performance is affected.

For the purpose of discussing body-control exercises, I divide the horse's body into three parts: the head and neck, the shoulders and torso, and the hindquarters. Obviously, every exercise described affects all parts of the horse's body. The drills, however, are classified according to the one part each develops the most.

These exercises are best introduced to the horse through a smooth snaffle bit. I do not recommend moving on to a curb bit until they are mastered in the mild snaffle, thus ensuring suppleness and the maturity to handle the leverage action of the curb.

ON THE BIT

The doorway to the control of a horse's body is his mouth. Through it, you gain control of the poll, the neck, the shoulders, the torso, and the hindquarters.

On the bit describes a horse who relaxes his jaw and flexes at the poll when light pressure is applied to his mouth. The horse who is on the bit draws his hocks under his body by rounding his back and lowering his croup. The result is an ability to elevate the forehand and move in balance on loose reins.

Although the body position of a horse on the bit may vary depending on the level of training and the maneuver performed, the basic elements of balance are still present. The horse spinning with his inside leg deep under his body and on loose reins is as round in the back and light in the forehand as the horse who moves in a balanced lope and loose reins on the rail.

An enhancement of the horse's response to the aids, being on the bit is necessary to soft upward and downward transitions, smooth turn-arounds, and straight and correct back ups. It is also fundamental to flying lead changes and all other maneuvers, whether a turn around the barrel or the reining horse's sliding stop.

Your horse will not be fully on the bit until he can perform at the walk, trot, and lope all the exercises included in this chapter. Once a horse is on the bit, continuous work on the suppling exercises is required to maintain the level of responsiveness, suppleness, and strength.

The Aids

Begin the process by driving your horse on the bit at the walk and in a straight line. Apply very light, delicate pressure to the horse's mouth as you drive him forward in the bridle with your legs and seat until he breaks at the poll. At the slightest flexion of the poll, open your fingers and release mouth and legs, letting the horse walk on freely as a reward. Let him walk a few strides and ask again. Be patient, gentle, and consistent. Feel carefully for your horse's response. As you become confident and your horse becomes more responsive, ask for more strides on the bit.

At this stage, do not release the reins completely when the horse gives at the poll. Rather, maintain a steady contact and let the horse find the most comfortable light-contact position. He should flex very slightly at the poll and tip his nose somewhat, rewarding himself rather than you having to move your hands forward. Repeat the exercise several times each session until your horse flexes at the poll as soon as you begin to drive and lift the slack out of the reins, holding his position until you turn the reins loose. Because you are seeking to build suppleness, softness, and confidence., never see-saw or jerk on your horse's mouth. Such actions can cause pain and stiffening through resistance.

As your horse builds confidence and suppleness, and you gain coordination and feel, do the same drill at the jog or trot.

After five to ten days in this exercise program, your horse should flex readily at the walk and jog. Likewise, you should be able to feel him give and move forward freely while on the

This horse walks forward on the bit in response to the light weight of the reins. (Photo: Ted Gard)

bit. Then proceed to apply the same lessons at the lope.

The action of setting the horse on the bit must come from your legs and hands if it is to be useful later in executing advanced maneuvers. Many riders make excessive use of side reins or otherwise tie their horse's head back to the saddle, causing the horse to get behind the bit. Because such flexion at the poll is not brought about by the rider's legs driving the horse on the bit, its only effect on the horse's body is on the poll and the neck. The result is a horse with a stiff back and torso, hindquarters that do not engage, and a rubber neck and poll to guide him. It is hardly possible to keep such a horse from dropping a shoulder into a barrel, picking up a wrong lead in a pleasure class, or missing a flying-lead change in a western riding class. Add bouncy spins and stops, crooked back ups, etc. Everything is affected.

SHOULDER CONTROL

In the turn around the first barrel, your horse runs wide because his shoulders drift to the outside. In the turn around the second barrel, he hits the barrel because he drops his shoulder into the turn.

Your pleasure horse's nose is out, his shoulder drops in toward the center of the pen. He cuts across the corner of the arena. Your cutting horse pushes his shoulder toward the cow when she runs across the pen on his right side. He leaks out and away from the herd. You have to pick up on the reins—a costly correction.

The shoulder takes the horse where he is going. This is why controlling it is so important. The more control you have of your horse's shoulders, the easier it is to guide your horse and the more accurate and refined you can be with your aids. Although both can be built at the same time, complete control of the shoulders is a prerequisite to full control of the hindquarters.

The shoulders are said to be "in," or "down," when they are to the inside of a straight line drawn from the horse's nose to

the tail set. If the head is to the right and the shoulder is to the left as the horse circles to the left, then the shoulder is "in," or "down," into the turn. If the head is to the right and the shoulder is to the left of a straight line from the nose to the tail set as the horse circles to the right, then the shoulder is said to be "out," or "up."

Shoulder control is developed through the practice of two exercises: the shoulder-up (small circle) drill, and guiding. The shoulder-up is called a drill to emphasize the fact that it is a suppling and control exercise only, not an end product. Guiding is both a control exercise and an end product of the well-schooled horse.

Shoulder-up

The shoulder-up drill is a forward movement during which the horse is bent in the direction of travel. As he performs the exercise to the right, your horse's spine is bent to the right, from the poll down through the neck, shoulders, and torso, all the way to the croup. His head is to the inside of the circle. There is a definite bend in his rib cage as he contracts and shortens the right side and relaxes the left. As he moves, your horse's hind feet track the same circle as his front feet.

There are two stages to the development of the shoulder-up drill. In the first stage, you concern yourself only with the lateral bend. In the advanced stage, both hands and both legs are used as the horse executes the drill while flexed at the poll and on the bit.

The Aids

To bring your horse into a shoulder-up drill to the right, apply a direct rein of opposition to the right. This rein effect brings your horse's head around to that side. Your left hand must release the left rein completely, allowing your horse to bend as much as possible.

If your horse tends to turn a very small circle rather than bending in the rib cage, use a right displacing leg at the cinch. The displacing leg holds the horse's shoulders and torso up and out while you bend the horse's spine around it with your outside leg back behind the cinch.

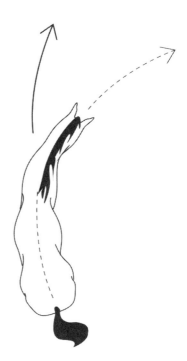

The aids for elementary shoulder-up. (1) Direct rein of opposition with the inside hand. (2) Use your outside leg to keep your horse's hindquarters from swinging out and to encourage him to bend in the body. Use your inside leg at the cinch if your horse tends to fall in, or your outside leg at the cinch if he tends to fall out.

This illustration shows a horse who is allowed to fall out of the circle—following the solid line. His shoulders are not moving toward his mouth; consequently, he will learn to evade the bit rather than move onto it while bent in the body. Were the horse not falling out of the circle, his shoulders would be moving in the direction of the dotted line.

Performing the advanced stage of shoulder-up, this horse is bent through the body and flexed at the poll. His shoulders are moving toward his mouth, a sure sign that he is not falling out of the circle. His hind feet are tracking in the same circle as his front feet. (Photo: Ted Gard)

It is very important that the aids be applied in an intermittent fashion. Bring the horse's nose to the right as you apply left leg pressure behind the cinch. As the horse gives to the light rein pressure and bends around your inside leg, remove the aids. The stiff horse will immediately take his head away and drop his shoulder and ribcage into the direction of the turn. Immediately, gently pick up on the rein and bring his head to the inside again as you again apply inside leg pressure at the cinch and outside leg behind the cinch. It is the simple principle of reward and reprimand. If you hold the horse's head in the same position, he eventually will pull against you and will become dull in the mouth. If you move his head and shoulders and then release the pressure, he will soon learn the benefits of responding to the aids. Once your horse bends readily in the rib cage on both sides, he is ready for the next stage.

In the advanced stage, apply contact with both reins—your outside leg behind the cinch and a light inside leg at the cinch. It is during this

The advanced shoulder-up seen from above. Notice the obvious bend in the horse's torso as evidenced by the outside of the horse being longer than the inside. (Photo: Ted Gard)

stage of the shoulder-up drill that you truly begin to pick up your horse's shoulders. By using both legs to drive the horse on the bit, you bring your horse to flex at the poll, engage his hind legs deep under himself, notably the inside hind leg, and carry more of his weight on his hind legs, thereby lightening up in the forequarters.

The shoulder-up drill is profitable for the performance horse in several ways: He learns to give softly to the direct rein of opposition and to let the rider put his head well to the inside of the circle. He also learns to move his shoulders and torso away from the rider's leg pressure at the cinch. This is important when the legs are used for directional purposes in training for circles, rollbacks, or spins, or when a holding leg is applied to position or steady the front quarters in such exercises as haunches-in and half-pass.

The shoulder-up drill supples and stretches the muscles of the horse's neck, shoulders, torso, and hip. This suppleness and elasticity enable the horse to turn either way without having to drop his shoulders into the turn. The result is more freedom during the turn and better form at a greater speed.

One word of caution about the shoulder-up drill: Do not let your horse's shoulders fall out of the small circle. Remember, your horse must be moving forward with a bent torso. A bent neck and straight torso often leads to the more

serious problem of a rubber neck and little control. So be sure your horse is tracking forward with his shoulders and not toward the outside of the circle.

Once you have gained the feel of walking and trotting your horse in a correct shoulder-up drill, you are well on your way to gaining control of your aids.

Guiding

Guiding is a key component of shoulder control. Not only does it indicate that you have sufficient control of your horse's shoulders to turn him, but also it is in itself an excellent way of developing that control. As you learn to coordinate your aids for guiding through turns, you also learn to guide your horse on a straight line.

The guiding horse keeps his body straight or slightly bent in the direction of the turn as he responds to a very light, loose outside rein on the side of his neck. Good guiding response gives you the ultimate control as to where you and your horse are headed next, whether at the lope or a fast gallop.

Many riders begin to work on guiding from a circle. The circle demands a great deal of guiding and is often too difficult for the rider, or horse, to perform correctly. Learn to guide by asking your horse to deviate slightly while walking or trotting straight lines across the pasture or riding area. The very small degree of turn is easy for your horse to perform and you can build on it all the way to a sharp and fast turn, such as those necessary for a winning barrel run.

The Aids

Applying good guiding aids is relatively simple. If your horse does not guide very well, or if you are uncertain of your guiding aids, begin with one hand on each rein. Use a mild snaffle and regular reins.

Put your horse at a walk or trot on a straight line in a large open area, such as a pasture. Be sure your horse is tracking straight and holding his body straight from poll to tail. Then slowly and gently take the slack out of the left rein by moving your left hand toward your belt buckle and above the center of the horse's neck. If your horse responds by changing direction, even only slightly, he has a basic knowledge of guiding. Release the aid and let him go straight for a few strides before asking for more turn.

If your horse does not respond, you need to school him in guiding as you learn it yourself. Rather than dropping the left rein aid, hold it in place as you take contact with the inside rein and effect an opening rein. The inside opening rein gives your horse direction. Hold the outside rein tight enough so your horse does not bend in the neck. A slack outside rein and a strong inside rein allow the horse to respond by bending his neck and falling out with the shoulders—the exact opposite of guiding and shoulder control, and the very thing you are trying to avoid. Reinforce your originally light neck-rein cue and inside opening rein with an outside reinforcing leg at the front cinch or forearm.

Feel for a *very slight* deviation in the line of travel. As soon as you feel it, release all the aids and let your horse travel freely in a straight line. Ask again.

Think of your outside rein and outside leg as a wall against which your horse bounces lightly, consequently forcing him to change direction.

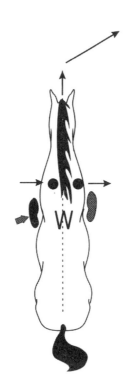

The aids to reinforce the light guiding neck rein. (1) opening with the inside hand, (2) equal contact with the outside neck rein and inside rein, (3) outside reinforcing leg at the cinch or shoulder.

Ask for slight deviations to the right until you get three or four good responses to the light outside rein, then change direction. Repeat the same procedure to the left. As you and your horse gain experience at guiding, move from an inside opening rein to a direct rein. The narrower distance between the reins is important if your horse is eventually going to guide one-handed.

Work on guiding in the same fashion until your horse responds to a light and loose outside rein with a strong deviation in the direction of travel. At this point, begin guiding work on the circles, using the same aids.

You can use the same guiding aids to teach your horse to travel in a straight line. Pick a landmark several hundred yards away and ride straight for it. Keep your eyes on the landmark and feel your horse as he moves. Feel your seat bones in the saddle, your thighs on each side of the skirting, your midsection as it moves in rhythm with your horse.

Then focus on whether your horse feels as though he is travelling straight to the landmark toward which you pointed him. Do you feel him deviate to the right without your requesting the turn? Simply apply the guiding aids as if you wanted to turn left until he is back in line with your target, then release the aids. With consistent correction your horse will soon learn to wait for your cues before changing direction.

The turn on the haunches is the result of guiding your horse in short straight lines and developing guiding responses to the point of ultimate shoulder control.

In developing and maintaining good guiding, the way you move your outside rein is important. Whether you are riding with two hands or only one-handed, the hand that holds the outside rein must move slowly when applying the rein on the horse's neck. The slow movement of your rein hand gives your horse the opportunity to feel the rein on his neck and respond correctly.

Also key to guiding is the fact that your outside-rein hand must never cross the center of the horse's neck. Crossing the center of the horse's neck with your neck-rein hand is a bad habit that results in pulling on the rein and forcing the horse's head to the outside of the turn.

It is an indication that you do not know how to correct the horse for poor response to the neck rein and will achieve poor guiding at best.

HINDQUARTER CONTROL

To fully develop your horse's potential, you must also gain control of his hindquarters. Without complete responsiveness and suppleness of his hindquarters, your horse's performance in executing lope departure, turn-arounds, circles, straight lines, upward and downward transitions, back ups, stops, flying-lead changes, and all other maneuvers will be marginal at best. Yet this level of performance is unattainable if you do not understand the coordination of the aids involved in gaining control of the hindquarters. I cannot overemphasize the importance of practicing these maneuvers properly, as they are part of the essential foundation of any specialized training.

Nowhere in all of horsemanship is the independent seat so important, however, as in the development of hindquarter control. If you are weak in this area of horsemanship, be sure to go back to the exercises detailed in chapter 4 (The Independent Seat). To go on without an independent seat will only lead to frustration on your part and confusion on the part of your horse.

Pivot on Forehand

The pivot on the forehand is the most basic of lateral movements. In performing it, the horse moves his hind legs in a circle with one foreleg acting as the pivot foot. It is a movement with very little forward motion. It is used to introduce the horse to the displacing leg. Because of its simplicity, the turn on the forehand can be introduced very early in the horse's training program. It requires only that a horse be relaxed and that he trust his rider.

In a turn on the forehand to the right, your horse's left front leg is the pivot limb. His left hind leg crosses under his belly and in front of the right hind leg. The horse's right front leg

takes very short steps and the right hind moves away in large side steps to the right. The horse's body is either straight or very slightly bent in the direction of the turn.

Using the corner of a fence is the best way to make this new maneuver easy for yourself and your green horse. Ride your horse along the fence until his nose gets to the corner. Stop him and stand for two or three minutes. Apply a displacing leg to the horse and move his hindquarters away from the closest fence and toward the other one. When the horse takes a step or two away from your leg, release the pressure and let him stand still.

Move the horse's hindquarters left and right, from one fence to the other, always waiting two or three minutes between each opposite movement. Failure to do so will cause the horse to become anxious. Anxiety hinders training, as the horse's mind is not concentrating on the aids.

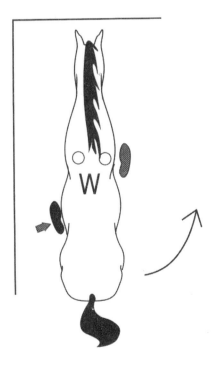

Introduce your horse to the displacing leg and pivot on the forehand by using the corner fence of your riding pen. (1) Ride your horse along the fence until his head is in the corner. (2) Maintain the position through very light contact of the reins on each side of the horse's neck. (3) Your right leg is passive at the cinch. (4) Apply your left displacing leg to move your horse's hindquarters to the right.

When your horse moves his hindquarters away from very light leg pressure, without trying to go forward or back, neither left nor right with his shoulders, he is ready to practice the maneuver in the open. At this time, coordination and balance of your aids are very important because your horse may move his front quarters in four different directions. For this reason, the pivot on the forehand is very profitable to you. You need to focus on how your horse feels to you and what he is doing with all four legs. If you feel your horse lean forward, subtly increase the pressure on the reins to keep him from moving. If you feel him lean back and want to back up, squeeze both legs slightly to balance him forward.

Leg-yield

Leg-yielding is a sideways movement in which the horse moves away from the rider's leg. Next to the pivot on the forehand, the leg-yield is a basic lateral movement and should be included in the training of the horse before he is ready for collected maneuvers.

In a leg-yield to the right, the horse's left legs cross sideways in front of the right legs. The horse's body is straight except for a very slight bend in the most forward part of the horse's neck—just enough of a bend for the rider to see the horse's left eyebrow.

The correct practice of leg-yielding will substantiate your ability to sit and use your leg aids effectively. Mentally, it will confirm for your horse his response to your displacing leg. It will loosen his shoulder and stifle joints and lay the groundwork for collection.

To help yourself and your horse leg-yield, begin by using the wall or fence. When your horse has mastered the exercise along the rail, ask for it in the open. Leg-yield to the right a few steps, ride straight a few steps, then leg-yield to the left a few steps. To increase your effective control over your horse's hindquarters and maximize the suppleness of his joints, practice leg-yielding at the trot.

The aids for leg-yielding to the right. (1) Ride your horse forward with the seat. (2) Apply a left displacing leg behind the cinch to push the hindquarters to the right. (3) Apply a light holding leg at the cinch to support the shoulders and maintain forward motion. (4) Establish contact at the mouth with two direct reins, to support the shoulders and keep the horse straight.

This horse's body is straight as he leg-yields to the left. Too much bend in the horse's body is the most common fault seen in leg-yielding. The problem occurs when a rider applies too much pressure with the hands and not enough pressure with the displacing and holding legs. (Photo: Ted Gard)

Haunches-in

The haunches-in is a lateral movement during which the hindquarters are brought in from the track and the horse's body is bent around the rider's inside leg.

The haunches-in is best introduced only after the horse has achieved a certain degree of collection, readily flexes at the poll, and has mastered the response to the shoulder-up and guiding aids. Once the horse responds to the displacing leg cue during the execution of the pivot on the forehand and the leg-yield, the haunches-in is simply the next logical step.

In a haunches-in to the right, the horse's neck and head are parallel to the direction of travel. The shoulders and rib cage are bent around the rider's right leg. The hindquarters are tracking to the right of the front legs. The horse's left hind leg moves forward and under the horse to cross in front of the right hind.

The haunches-in is very useful in developing collection. It prepares the horse for smooth lead

departure and soft flying-lead changes. Practicing the haunches-in results in better control of the horse in circles, stops, back ups, and turn-arounds.

Begin your practice of the haunches-in by using the rail. Establish flexion at the poll, then apply the seat and leg aids. Do not expect too much at first. A slight lateral movement of the hindquarters over one or two steps is all you should ask for. When you get such a response, drop the aids and let the horse walk on the rail. Ask again later. As the horse gains ability, expect more lateral movement on a longer distance.

As you apply your aids, feel for the horse's response. His haunches will move away from your outside leg. His forward rhythm should not change. He should not slow down or speed up but rather remain soft on the bit.

The aids for a haunches-in to the right. (1) Ride the horse into the movement with a driving seat. (2) Apply a right holding leg at the cinch to maintain forward motion and bend the horse. (3) Alternate between direct rein and indirect rein of opposition to hold the horse's shoulders on the line of travel. (4) Apply a left displacing leg behind the cinch to move the hindquarters to the right of the line of travel. (5) Use the left rein as a direct rein to regulate the bend and to maintain collection.

Haunches-in viewed from above. The horse is travelling in straight line with his mane. (Photo: Ted Gard)

Too much angle during haunches-in. The benefits of suppling and collection are lost because the horse is forced to step sideways with his hind legs rather than under himself. (Photo: Ted Gard)

Because the horse will learn to rely on the fence or wall, school him in the open as soon as he performs well along the fence. Practice the haunches-in at the trot and lope to develop suppleness and collection.

The Half-pass

The half-pass is a forward and sideways movement on two tracks, in which the horse is very

Haunches-in at the trot. The horse travels in a straight line with the camera. Her hindquarters are to the right of the line of travel and her outside hind leg travels in the same track as her inside front. (Photo: Ted Gard)

slightly bent through his body in the direction of the movement. The half-pass is performed at a walk, trot, or lope. It is best introduced only after the horse has achieved a strong foundation of suppleness, collection, and responsiveness through the practice of the leg-yield and the haunches-in.

The half-pass will further develop control of the horse's body, particularly when practiced at the trot and lope. By maximizing suppleness of the stifle and hip joint, a rider will be able to bring the horse to the even greater degree of collection necessary for events such as western pleasure, western riding, and reining.

When performing a half-pass to the right, your horse's body is bent to the right. His shoulders lead his hindquarters very slightly. His left legs cross in front of his right legs. Your horse is flexed at the poll and collected. The degree of sideways movement depends on the amount of training your horse has received, the level of collection he has attained, and his athletic ability.

Forward motion, or impulsion, must be paramount in your mind when riding a half-pass. You must correct any loss of impulsion immediately by letting the hindquarters fall behind until forward motion is regained. Then ask your horse for more sideways movement as his collection improves.

We often see a horse perform a half-pass while his body is bent in the opposite direction of the course of travel. This fault stems from the rider's lack of understanding of the half-pass and a lack of preparation of his horse for the maneuver. Another fault brought about by lack of preparation is lagging hindquarters. This fault indicates a lack of responsiveness to the displacing leg and can be corrected by a return to the leg-yield exercise.

The Sidepass

The sidepass is a lateral movement during which the line of travel is at a right angle to the longitudinal axis of the horse. Once your horse has mastered the haunches-in and the half-pass, he will perform the sidepass without the need for further training. It becomes a simple matter of eliminating forward motion by applying more pressure on the reins and dispensing with the holding leg at the girth.

The most common fault in sidepassing is seen in the positioning of the horse's body. Many riders bend their horses away from the direction of travel. They fail to develop the horse's responsiveness to the displacing leg. Furthermore, they allow their horses to drop their shoulders into the sidepass. In a sidepass to the right, for example, the rider can correct the fault by applying more rein pressure with the right hand to hold the shoulders back and more leg pressure on the left side to move the hindquarters faster.

Many riders use the sidepass as a means of training horses to move away from the legs. Although this practice is not wrong, it has very limited benefits. Since the sidepass offers no forward movement, it is useless in developing a

horse's ability to collect. Therefore, it is much more beneficial to the horse's performance if a rider develops the pivot on the forehand, leg-yield, haunches-in, and half-pass and considers the sidepass as a by-product rather than a means to an end.

The correct sidepass: the horse's body is straight from poll to croup, the rider sits upright, not leaning inside or outside of the movement.

The aids for a sidepass to the left. (1) The right displacing leg moves the horse's body to the left. (2) The left leg is clear away from the horse's body. (3) The hands apply the necessary amount of pressure to the mouth to restrict forward motion. (4) The right neck rein touches the horse's neck, moving the front quarters to the left. The horse's body is straight. The right legs cross over the left legs as the horse moves to the left.

Back Up as a Suppling Exercise

Suppling the horse while backing up is a very effective way of gaining body control of your horse. It demands good control over your aids and offers a great opportunity to develop slow, sensitive hands.

Suppling your horse during back up develops strength in his back and hindquarters. It reinforces his ability to engage his hindquarters and elevate his withers—a skill essential to many performance events.

The aids are very much the same as for the haunches-in. Ride your horse forward on the bit at the walk. Take your legs away from his sides, say "whoa," and hold the contact until he gives. Once he gives to the bit, release the reins slowly until they are loose. Then slowly lift the slack out of the reins. Once you can feel your horse's mouth, gently squeeze your legs and back him up in a straight line, with his hindquarters either to the left or the right of the line of travel

The aids for back up as a suppling exercise. Right or left, the aids are essentially the same as for haunches-in except that the hands act before the legs, thereby engaging the horse into a back up.

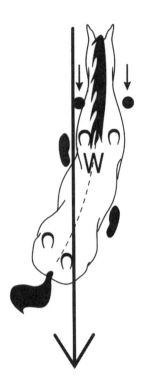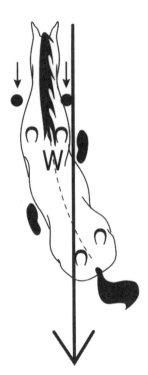

CHAPTER 15

Western Pleasure and Trail

"A good western pleasure horse . . . should have a balanced, flowing motion."

—*AQHA Handbook*

Western pleasure is the most popular of all western horsemanship events. The reason for such popularity is that western pleasure schooling, both for the horse and the rider, is well-suited to a host of other events. Indeed trail, western riding, horsemanship, equitation, and even hunter hack are based on western pleasure balance, movement, and frame.

Implied in the following discussion of western pleasure and trail is the fact that you and your horse are working on, and mastering, the body-control exercises described in chapter 14. Without these exercises, your western pleasure horse will be negatively affected by your lack of expertise in applying effective aids and your inability to position his body for optimum performance. Clearly, body control is essential to the trail horse. How can a rider hope to negotiate the trail obstacles precisely and fluidly without the kind of control those exercises afford? I therefore point to body-control exercises as a way of correcting your horse or of positioning him for certain parts of the event.

In the western pleasure section, I discuss the important element of balance at the walk, trot, and lope. I also describe how to coordinate your aids for the key upward and downward transitions. I talk about leads, why they are important, and how to feel them. And finally, I give you some tips on getting your western pleasure horse shown.

In the trail section, I detail some important principles of riding trail obstacles. I also explain how to coordinate your aids to negotiate the three most popular and most encompassing obstacles: the gate, the back-through, and the sidepass over an obstacle.

WESTERN PLEASURE

Western pleasure is a quiet event in which emphasis is placed on balance and correctness of movements. Therefore, your aids and approach to schooling must be focused on maintaining a happy, quiet mind in your horse. The western pleasure horse never gets to the point of doing things quickly. A steady assurance that your horse will respond is the correct mental approach you must take.

Winning western pleasure performance begins with your feel for balance and correct movement. You can develop this feel by studying the horse's three gaits and the sequence of leg and weight shift. Watching horses move, and riding many different horses to experience their gaits and levels of balance, are also essential to developing a feel for balance. But what is most important is riding balanced horses. If you do not have access to balanced horses, work with a western pleasure trainer or coach and create an opportunity to exercise their horses.

Let's see how to coordinate your aids to achieve balance at the walk, trot, and lope.

Balance at the Walk, Trot, and Lope

The balanced western pleasure horse, much like the horse on the bit, drives forward with his hindquarters deep under himself. His back is round and up under the saddle. His forehand is elevated. His stride is fluid and of good length. His poll is level with his withers. The bridge of his nose is either vertical to the ground or slightly ahead of the vertical. The horse maintains this balanced frame on the very light contact of safely loose reins.

Regulations call for severe faults when a horse carries his poll so low that the tips of his ears are lower than his withers. Other severe faults include the head carried too high, over-flexed at the poll behind the vertical, reins too long, quick or choppy stride, and a horse that appears lethargic and emaciated.

The aids for balance at all three gaits are the same as those used to put a horse on the bit. Drive your horse forward into the bridle with your seat and leg aids as you hold him with your hands until he lowers his head and loosens the reins. Be sure your reins are adjusted so that your horse finds relief from the aids before his head gets too low. And give your pleasure horse plenty of time to respond to the aids. This principle is important when schooling for any event, but even more so with the western pleasure horse. Remember, you want to end up with a confident, responsive, but quiet horse.

Avoid using severe bits and doing a great deal of see-sawing on the bit. This "head-setting" approach destroys your horse's confidence. As he worries about his head and finds a comfortable place to bury his mouth, he learns to move behind the bit with the bridge of his nose behind the vertical and his head much too low for balanced movement. The low head results in a horse on the forehand rather than one elevated in the shoulders and round in the back under your saddle. An approach that consists of too much hands and not enough driving aids leaves you with a horse whose head is set but whose body is not balanced. In other words, the rhythm of footfall at the walk, trot, and lope is not natural.

Begin with the walk. Ride your horse forward and relaxed, working on suppling exercises and control. Ride a sufficient amount of walk to learn to feel a steady rhythm. The walk is important because a forward yet steady pace will make it easier for the horse to move into correct transitions. Do not overschool your horse's head position. As long as it is not too high, let him find a comfortable and relaxed place to carry it.

Then move into a jog and focus on keeping your horse relaxed and in rhythm rather than exceedingly slow. Keep your horse moving with your legs, using as little hand as possible to slow him down. Again, using the hands too much destroys the naturally diagonal gait. Your

Ridden by Cindy Soderberg, MCR Frosty Friday shows the form that earned her the QHAA Hi-point two-year-old western pleasure in 1990. Her level topline, medium flexion at the poll, and balanced jog stride depict the frame sought after by successful western pleasure trainers and judges. (Photo: Sharon Latimer)

horse's front leg eventually touches the ground before his diagonal hind leg rather than at the same time. It is as if your absentee legs are not bringing your horse's hind legs up at the same speed as the front legs. Consequently, the hind legs are taking shorter strides and the true gait is lost. This easily recognized lack of balance is considered a serious fault in western pleasure and is marked accordingly.

Now walk again for a few minutes and then move your horse into a lope. Use just enough leg and seat aids to drive the horse forward at the lope without breaking into a trot. If your horse is a touch fast, he is either stiff or not relaxed enough. In the case of stiffness, continue to work on suppling and body-control exercises. If the problem is one of fear, more loping with very soft aids and giving your horse plenty of time to respond will eventually allow him to relax.

Again, use enough driving aids so that your horse maintains impulsion. Using too much hands to slow him down and not enough leg to drive his hindquarters under him leads to a lack of balance and a loss of natural gait. Your

horse's inside hind leg eventually touches the ground after his outside front rather than at the same time. Besides being a serious fault that results in serious consequences to the score you get at the show, this fault renders your horse very unsafe to ride.

Continue to school your horse, blending in body-control exercises with the showlike conditions of western pleasure. Continue to focus on your seat, position, and the effectiveness of your aids. Ride as many horses as you can. When you ride one that walks, jogs, lopes on loose reins, never gains speed, has a distinct natural beat to each gait, and feels like a rocking chair, memorize the feeling, for that is the feel you want on every western pleasure horse.

Transitions

Transitions are the changes from one gait to another. Upward transitions are changes from a slow gait to a faster one. Downward transitions are changes from a faster to a slower gait. A transition from the lope to the jog is a downward transition, for example, as is the transition from a gallop to a lope.

Transitions are where many western pleasure classes are won or lost. Indeed, it takes a certain measure of skills to ride correctly on the rail at a steady pace, but advanced feel and coordination are required to effect smooth and balanced transitions.

Fundamental to fluid, smooth transitions are the complete body-control exercises described in chapter 14. Clearly, this does not mean that you wait until your horse performs the exercises correctly before doing transitions. It does mean, however, that the key to transitions is body control.

Every transition is based on your horse's ability to go on the bit, because for a smooth transition you must be able to balance your horse. A horse that has not been schooled to go on the bit without resistance is on his forehand. It will be difficult for you to have him round his back under the saddle, bring his hind legs deep under himself, and elevate his forehand for upward and downward transitions.

To ride a walk-to-jog transition, make contact with your horse's mouth to balance him, squeezing both legs to drive him forward with more impulsion.

Although more demanding, the walk-to-lope transition is nevertheless a good test of your feel for your horse's position and response. Establish light contact with your horse's mouth and even contact from both impulsion legs at the cinch. This combination of aids places your horse in a forward mode and lets him know you are about to ask for a balanced movement. Once your horse is forward and flexed at the poll, leaving you with a "soft butter" feel in your hands, he is ready for the transition. Keeping equal weight on each of your seat bones, sit tall with your shoulder blades close to each other. Place your inside leg at the front cinch and move your horse's shoulders out very slightly. Feel your horse's mouth with both reins to keep his forehand elevated, and press with your outside leg behind the cinch to move his hindquarters inside the line of travel. Feel his body position as he bends in the spine around your inside leg. Now press with both legs and lope.

Positioning the horse for a walk-to-lope transition. The horse's hindquarters are to the inside of the line of travel. The horse is bent around the rider's inside leg. He is flexed at the poll and on the bit.

If you schooled your horse in body control and you applied the correct aids, he should have loped off without rooting his nose out, raising his head, or galloping fast and unbalanced.

Downward transitions are very much dependent on your horse's responsiveness to seat aids. To ride down from a lope to a walk, or a jog to a walk, pick up on the reins softly. As you make soft contact with the mouth, squeeze your legs gently to collect your horse. As you feel your horse engage his hind legs deeper under himself, apply a holding seat until your horse responds and goes through the transition forward and on the bit. There should be no pushing against the bit and no change of rhythm.

Correct transitions are possible only when you have complete control of your aids through an independent seat. Your horse's transitions, just like the rest of his performance, will be fluid and smooth only if your aids are imperceptible, precise, and consistent. If your aids are sudden, harsh, overly strong, or too weak, your horse's transitions will reflect those characteristics.

Not only do you need to be in complete control of your aids, but you must also be able to feel what your horse is about to do before he does it. In other words, you must be able to assess how your horse is responding to your aids as you apply them. Is he going on the bit as he should, or is he bracing against the bit? Is he pushing against your inside leg and actually moving his shoulders into it? Is he moving his hindquarters away from your outside leg? And above all, in the walk-to-lope transitions, is he about to pick up the correct lead?

Leads

The term lead refers to the loping stride. We say that the horse is on the left lead when the left front reaches farther ahead than the right front, and vice versa. Leads are a basic yet very important aspect of horsemanship. In fact, leads are key whether you are riding western pleasure, reining, barrel racing, or cutting.

Beginner riders often have difficulty identifying which lead their horses are loping on. Yet it does not have to be this way. Any rider with at least twenty hours of experience riding at the lope should be able to identify, without any difficulty, which lead his or her horse is on. A simple way to learn how to feel which lead your horse is using is described next.

Let's begin with a review of the lope stride. As you may recall, chapter 8 described the lope as a three-beat gait. When your horse lopes on the left lead, he pushes with the right hind, lands on the left hind and right front for the second beat of the stride, and finally places his weight on the left front before going into suspension. In the process of the stride, your horse's inside feet, in this case the left ones, touch the ground ahead of the outside feet. This allows your horse to lean slightly in the direction of the left turn for balance.

The problems begin when your horse is loping on the left lead but turning to the right. Such a horse is said to be on the wrong lead. His outside feet touch the ground farther ahead than his inside feet. This poses a balance problem for the horse, making it difficult for him to lean slightly in the direction of the turn. The other difficulty is that your horse pushes himself with his inside hind leg rather than his outside hind leg (as he does when on the correct lead). Pushing with his inside hind leg forces the horse to turn on his forehand and makes it impossible for him to turn a small circle. If a small circle is attempted anyway, your horse is likely to slip and fall. Thus, for safety and performance reasons, it is vital that you be able to feel on which lead your horse is loping or galloping.

The method is simple. When your horse is on the correct lead, he pushes with his outside hind leg and the movement of his body is directed smoothly from back to front. Therefore, your seat bones would tend to slide in a straight line from the back of your seat to the front of it. When your horse is on the wrong lead, he pushes with his inside hind leg. This forces his hindquarters to swing out from the inside of the circle to the outside of it. Take some time and observe a horse loping a circle on the wrong lead. Notice this movement of his hindquarters every time he takes a stride. This inside-to-outside swing is communicated to the horse's

back, the saddle, and your seat. Consequently, when loping on the wrong lead, your seat bones—instead of sliding smoothly from the back to the front—are forced from the inside to the outside of the saddle.

Learning to feel correct and wrong leads depends on your focusing on your seat and how it moves in the saddle. Every time your horse lopes, ask yourself: "Which lead is my horse on?" Have your coach or someone else verify that you correctly identified the lead. If your horse is on the wrong lead, gently bring him down to a walk or jog and ask again.

Many riders try to identify the leads by looking at the horse's shoulders. According to this method, the horse is on the left lead when the left shoulder is farther forward than the right one. This method presents a number of difficulties: (1) You do not learn to feel your horse through your seat if you depend on your eyes to ride. (2) Feeling the leads through your seat enables you eventually to feel which lead your horse will pick up before he lopes. (This is important in preventing horses from loping on the wrong lead.) (3) Identifying the leads by looking at the horse's shoulders forces you to lean forward, taking your seat out of the saddle and rendering your aids ineffective. In addition, your leaning forward loads your horse's forehand, making it even more difficult for him to lope off on the correct lead.

Learn to feel the leads through your seat and, as a result, your effectiveness at other maneuvers will improve.

Showing Your Western Pleasure Horse

Correct body position, effective yet subtle aids, and a well-schooled horse are all essential to winning western pleasure. But none of those factors will help if you do not show your horse at his best. In the rest of this western pleasure section, I give you some tips on showing your western pleasure horse successfully. I discuss the arena footing, how to position yourself in the class, passing other horses, negotiating corners, reversing, and backing.

Naturally, the best place to ride your western pleasure horse is right along the rail. The rail in many show rings, however, gets hard and carved in after a number of rail classes. The hard ground does not offer much cushioning for your horse's feet and legs and the uneven, rounded track along the rail can cause him to appear sore. Therefore, if you show your horse in these conditions, guide him just inside the track along the rail.

Really deep ground also is detrimental to your horse's movements. In an effort to get his feet out of deep sand, your horse will show much more knee action than is desired in a western pleasure horse. If you can, avoid areas in which the footing is deeper than three or four inches.

It is easy to get lost in a crowded western pleasure class. Part of showing your horse is positioning him so that the judge can notice you. As you watch other horses warm up in the hitching ring, determine where you fit among the competition. If you think you are riding the best horse, place yourself next to the other "best" horses. If you feel that your horse is somewhere in the middle, in terms of calibre, avoid riding in the show ring next to someone whose horse is much more show ready. The calibre of his or her horse will make yours look as though it does not belong there.

Regardless of the calibre of horse you are riding, stay away from the problem horses in the class. Their speed, head tossing, or kicking often scares other horses.

Passing during a western pleasure class used to be considered taboo. If you had to pass you knew you would not place. Fortunately, those days are gone. As we let western pleasure horses move more naturally, the slowest horses are not necessarily the most desirable. Nevertheless, passing must be done with care so that you do not disturb your horse or the other horse's performance.

Be aware of the pace of the class and the other horses around you. This will help you plan ahead before you find yourself having to pass someone. You need to pass when your horse's head gets within seven or eight feet of the slower horse. Begin your move by looking over your shoulder to be sure that no other rider is passing you. Use your peripheral vision for this so that you do not make noticeable moves. If the way is clear, apply pressure with your outside leg at the cinch and a very subtle neck rein to your horse. Be sure to put a minimum of four feet between you and the slower horse. Any closer and you may endanger yourself and the other rider.

Continue in a straight line until your horse's tail is seven or eight feet ahead of the slow horse's head. Turn your head as little as possible and use your peripheral vision to determine your position. Turning your head too much looks bad and your horse may feel the twist in your body and begin to return to the rail too soon. Once your horse is far enough ahead of the slow horse, apply light inside leg pressure at the cinch and a very subtle inside neck rein to guide your horse back to the rail. Your horse should remain straight in the body and maintain his cadence all through the maneuver.

Riding corners effectively depends greatly upon your horse's response to a very subtle inside leg at the cinch and an inside rein on the neck, for these are the aids you need to apply to keep your horse from falling into the turn and losing his balanced frame. Indeed, as you approach the corner, but while your horse is still travelling straight, softly build a wall with your inside aids so that your horse can remain round in the back and elevated in the forehand all through the turn. As you might expect, he will respond only if you have schooled him in body control at home. Another thing about corners: learn how tight your horse can turn without losing balance, and do not ask him to turn any tighter. Remember, this is western pleasure, and picking up on the reins to rebalance your horse after a corner is no more acceptable there than anywhere else during the class.

Reversing is an opportunity to reposition yourself within the class. For instance, a sharp turn on the haunches and walk off on the rail can put some distance between you and the horse now behind you. A larger circle can help distance you from the horse now ahead of you. In either case, be sure your horse is responsive to guiding. He should respond to the very subtle neck rein without elevating his head or pushing against the bit.

Prepare your horse to back by shortening your reins as you get to the lineup. When the judge calls for your horse to back up, squeeze your knees and lift the reins slowly, allowing the horse time to begin his move. Sit upright and straight. Hold the contact with the aids and continue to back until the judge moves to the next horse.

Riding your western pleasure horse successfully is not easy by any means. But it is an attainable goal with plenty of rewards along the way.

TRAIL CLASS

Working on trail obstacles is a great way to develop feel for your horse and your aids. If done correctly, you gain increased confidence as a result of the relaxed cooperation between you and your horse. You feel more prepared for other kinds of events as your horse learns to respond accurately to your aids. And that is the challenge with trail: precision.

Addressing the trail class, *The American Quarter Horse Association's 1993 Official Handbook* reads:

> *This class will be judged on the performance of the horse over the obstacles, with emphasis on manners, response to the rider and attitude. Horse shall be penalized for any unnecessary delay while approaching the obstacles. . . . Credit will be given to those horses negotiating the obstacles with style and some degree of speed, providing carefulness is not sacrificed. Credit will be given to those horses showing capability of picking their own way through course when obstacles warrant it, and willingly responding to rider's cues on more difficult obstacles.*

It is not enough for the horse to walk through and over every obstacle; he must do it with style and in a responsive manner. This style and responsiveness is built upon the body-control foundation I discussed in chapter 14. And it is built upon some schooling principles that apply to the schooling of all horses but particularly to trail horses. Here are those principles:

1. Be sure all the materials you use for obstacles are safe for you and your horse. No nails, bolts, or any other sharp objects should be on the surface of the rails, bridge, gate, etc.

2. Even if your horse is not ready to start on obstacles, school him around them and ride close to them so that he gets used to the sight of them.

3. Be sure you have full body control of your horse before you start schooling on obstacles. Your horse needs to perform correctly and in a relaxed, confident manner the following maneuvers: pivot on the forehand, haunches-in, turn on the haunches, sidepass, and back-up as a suppling exercise. Begin work on obstacles without these movements and your lack of control over your horse's body will make it impossible for you to show him the correct way of negotiating the trail class.

4. Never discipline your horse over an obstacle because he will associate discipline with the obstacle and after awhile will approach it with anxiety and tension. If he refuses to move away from your leg, for instance, ride him away from the obstacle and work on body-control exercises. Once he responds again, take him back to the obstacle and continue schooling.

5. Take a great deal of time to go through an obstacle, never moving your horse more than two steps without standing still for at least one minute. Opening and closing a gate should take a minimum of eight to ten minutes. Backing through the L should take even longer. To build your confidence before the show, ride through the obstacle once or twice without stopping. This method of schooling

teaches your horse to wait for your cue for every step he takes while negotiating an obstacle. In other words, you control when your horse will move, which leg he will move, and where he will place his foot. This is very important because there will be times when the obstacles will be tight and your horse will need to depend on your guidance for correct performance. At home, regularly riding an obstacle without stopping encourages your horse to anticipate the process and go too fast.

6. Make obstacles an inviting and relaxing place for your horse by working on his gaits until he is ready for a break, then letting him rest while negotiating an obstacle.

7. Be sure to vary the order in which you negotiate the obstacles. Failure to do so will pattern your horse and, again, anticipation will spoil his performance in the show ring.

8. Always use the lightest, most subtle possible aids to negotiate an obstacle. Once his schooling is complete, your horse will look as though he is doing it on his own.

9. Use the word "whoa" as you let your horse stand every one or two steps. In addition to saying "whoa," place your rein hand on his withers and do not move it until you are ready to move him again. Soon you will be able to stop your horse simply by placing your rein hand on his withers. This cue comes in handy when you work on the back-through and numerous other obstacles: taking up on the reins to stop your horse from backing up will only cause him to back up farther and faster.

10. The trail class also requires you to show your horse at the walk, jog, and lope at various places between the obstacles as part of his work. Therefore, remember to focus on transitions, balanced gaits, and frame just as you would with your western pleasure horse. In fact, because you usually do not have a great deal of space between obstacles in which to perform at all three gaits, it is very important that your horse be able to move promptly and smoothly into the next gait. Trotting into a lope departure, for instance, may force you into the next obstacle without having had an opportunity to show your horse at the lope.

11. Introduce your horse to trail by using the simplest form of each obstacle. For example, begin work on walk-overs and sidepass with only one pole on the ground. Help yourself and your horse in the back-through by using only two rails, set at least four feet apart. Ride forward halfway between the rails and begin backing from there rather than going all the way through. Use a piece of heavy plywood on the ground as an introductory bridge. Do not move on to more sophisticated obstacles until your horse is comfortable with the simple ones and you are able to guide him through and over them correctly.

With these basic principles in mind, let's discuss aids to guide the horse through the most popular obstacles: the gate, the walk-overs, and the back-throughs.

The Gate

After years of judging horse shows, I am convinced that riders spend less time preparing their horses for the gate than for any other obstacle. Yet the gate need not be a source of lost points. Assuming that your horse responds well to the body-control exercises described in chapter 14, fifteen minutes of practicee a day for three weeks will be more than most horses and riders need to score high on the gate.

There are four ways to open and close a gate on horseback. The method I describe here is the most popular and the safest of all four. It is important that you use a gate made of solid material, such as wood or steel. Do not attempt to open a wire gate if you are on horseback.

Guide your horse parallel to the gate and close enough that your lower leg is approximately six inches away from the gate. Position your horse so that his head is past the gate opening and your hand can easily reach the latch. Although doing so is not necessarily more desirable, you may want to sidepass to the gate when showing your horse. Be sure you sit evenly on both seat bones and keep your upper body straight. Leaning over to open the gate forces your leg into the side of your horse and pushes him away from the gate.

Stop your horse's forward walk as soon as his hindquarters clear the gate. Execute a pivot on the forehand so that your horse's hindquarters move away from the opening but remain close to the gatepost. Swing the gate behind your leg, after which a turn on the haunches toward the gate lets you close and latch it shut without leaning over. (Photo: Ted Gard)

Unlatch the gate and back your horse up so that his head clears the gatepost. Push the gate open and guide your horse through, using a turn on the haunches. Remember to stop and stand every one or two steps.

This is how most riders handle the gate. The horse swings wide around the gate and leaves a large opening. This approach takes more time, does not look as tidy, and does not show as much control as the one described for the preceding figure.

Pay attention to your horse's reactions as you work through the gate. Is he fearful as you approach the gate? Ride him as close as you can and stand there for a while. If he is not right next to the gate and you would have to lean over to unlatch it, do not do it. He is not ready for you to ride him through yet and attempting to do so will lead either to an accident or to your horse becoming fearful. Is he getting nervous and tense once he is halfway through the gate? Many horses get tense at this stage and will try to rush through the gate if you let them. Stop and stand still for several minutes. Remember to stop and stand your horse for one or two minutes every two steps.

Walk-overs

Although they appear simple, walk-overs are quite demanding in the way of aids and control. Supportive, firm aids are necessary to encourage your horse initially to move on and over the obstacles.

Place one pole on the ground and walk your horse over the middle of it several times until he is comfortable with it. Next, trot your horse, and then lope him over the single pole. When he is comfortable with one pole, add another one, and so on. As you add poles, pay attention to the distance between them. For walk-overs, the poles should be set 15 inches to 24 inches apart. Jog-overs call for 3 feet to 3 feet 6 inches between poles, lope-overs, from 6 feet to 7 feet. Use heavy poles so that they do not move and lose position when your horse bumps them. This way, you do not have to dismount and reset the poles while schooling.

If your horse hesitates as he approaches the poles, squeeze him with your legs and drive him forward with your seat. Some horses may try to avoid walking over the pole by turning left or right. If this is the case, spread your hands wide and maintain light contact so that he cannot escape the middle of the pole.

If the poles are raised off the ground, lift your seat out of the saddle just enough to take your weight away from your horse's back and transfer it to your stirrups. This will allow your horse

Introduce your horse to walk-overs by riding him over a single pole.

to lift his back and bend his joints sufficiently to clear the poles.

Allow your horse to take a close look and even smell the poles if he lowers his head to them. This is an important step in building your horse's confidence in handling all sorts of walk-overs.

If your horse is constantly hitting poles, you may be the cause. Perhaps you are sitting too far back against the cantle of your saddle. Or you may be pulling on his mouth just as he steps over a pole, causing him to raise his head suddenly, hollow his back, and step low and short. Perhaps you are leaning forward and forcing him out of balance as he tries to pick his way through the rails. Or your aids may be too sudden and too strong, causing him to move with long strides in a tight and narrow obstacle. Once your horse maintains his balance at all three gaits over four to five poles, vary the shape of the obstacle by raising and lowering poles.

Is your horse fearful of stepping into water or over a bridge? Place his feed in such a way that he has to step over a piece of plywood or a puddle of water to get to it. Your horse will make up his own mind about the foreign object and next time you ride him up to it he will likely go over without a fuss. After the fear of the basic obstacle has disappeared, progress to a slightly raised bridge. Also be sure to ride your trail horse through all sorts of water obstacles. Stay away from metal water obstacles and those with other types of slippery bottoms. Puddles are safe for training your trail horse and easy to create.

Back-throughs

Back-throughs, a required part of trail classes, come in many forms. You may be asked to back your horse between three barrels, cones, or a number of rails arranged in L, V, or U shapes. The rails may be on the ground or they may be raised.

Again, the most important foundation to back-throughs is body control. In performing back-throughs, you will need your horse to execute turns on the haunches, pivots on the forehand, and back ups. You must be able to have your horse back up left and right and stop when you place your hand on his withers.

The aids for the back-through vary according to which stage of the obstacle you are riding. Entering the back-through likely requires a turn on the haunches. Turning the sharp corner of the obstacle calls for a few steps of pivot on the forehand alternating with the same amount of turn on the haunches. All through the obstacle,

your horse should be soft and responsive to your aids and flexed at the poll.

A successful back-through is one that has been approached correctly. Therefore, concentrate on approaching the obstacle quietly and in a relaxed manner. Here's how to do it: Imagine that the obstacle is on your right. Ride your horse perpendicular to the entrance of the obstacle, with the poles about ten inches from your horse's front feet. Stop your horse as his hind feet get to the center of the space between the poles. Using your right neck rein and your right leg at the cinch, move your horse into a turn on the haunches to the left until his body is in line with the poles. If your turn on the haunches was executed correctly, your horse is centered and ready to back up without a fault.

Difficulties with the back-through generally stem from the rider rushing the horse through the schooling and the obstacle. Tension and overreaction on the part of the horse result in his hitting the rail and tossing his head, and in uncontrolled backing. Another common fault is the rider's twisting of his or her body from left to right in an effort to locate the horse's position. This twisting causes your weight to shift constantly and your legs to bump the horse left and right. Your horse gets confusing signals and low marks on the obstacle.

Begin schooling back-throughs by riding your horse forward between two rails, stopping before you exit, then backing slowly, one step at a time. Your horse gets the opportunity to see the rails as he moves forward between them and feels more secure than he would if you started by trying to back him in.

Positioning the horse to enter the back-through. This rider stopped when her horse's hind feet were in the middle of the space between the two poles.

A horse that waits for you at every step is paramount when negotiating the corner. Alternate between a few steps of turn on the haunches, followed by a few steps of pivot on the forehand until your horse is past the corner.

Elevating the walk-overs helps keep your horse alert. He also learns to handle the obstacles based on your control rather than on habituation.

When you get to the show, relax your horse by practicing body control, establishing communication and reminding him of the expected responses. Work him at all three gaits, making sure that the transitions are as smooth as they were at home. Ride him all over the grounds to familiarize him with the sights and sounds of this particular horse show. Ask the show management if you can have a look at the obstacles and even walk the trail course (without your horse, naturally). Study the pattern and imagine yourself riding your horse through the course.

Trail is a precise event that demands patience and control. Plenty of quiet work on various obstacles develops your ability to coordinate and time your aids. And that puts you on the road to accomplished horsemanship.

The T obstacle is a good exercise in control. It calls for sidepasses, turns on the haunches, and turns on the forehand.

CHAPTER 16

Reining

"To rein a horse is not only to guide him but also to control his every movement."

Reining is one of the most challenging of all equine sports. Electrifying spins, smooth speed control, effortless lead changes, and magical sliding stops all contribute to make reining a very exciting event.

And reining is a demanding sport. There are several maneuvers to learn and a large combination of horsemanship skills necessary to perform them. On exhibiting a reining horse, the *National Reining Horse Association Judges' Guide* says:

> *To rein a horse is not only to guide him but also to control his every movement. The best reined horse should be willingly guided or controlled with little or no apparent resistance and dictated to completely. Any movement on his own must be considered a lack of control. All deviations from the exact written pattern must be considered a lack of or temporary loss of control; and therefore, a fault that must be marked down according to the severity of the deviation. . . . credit should be given for smoothness, finesse, attitude, quickness and authority of performing various maneuvers, while using controlled speed which raises the difficulty level and makes him more exciting and pleasing to watch to an audience.*

All of this demands a high measure of feel, one that takes years to attain.

You can go about developing the necessary reining feel in a number of ways. First, you must have an independent seat. For reasons outlined earlier in the book, an independent seat is paramount to advanced horsemanship, such as reining. Reining will come easier to you if you have a background in such balanced events as equitation, western pleasure, trail, and western riding. These slower events allow more time for performance and let you develop a feel for the general position and balance of your horse. Therefore, the more riding experience you have before you begin reining, the faster the sport will come to you. Also important to acquiring the feel of reining is a tremendous amount of regular, focused riding. Not necessarily riding reining horses, but many different horses. If you are the type of rider who enjoys riding no more than two or three times a week, you may never attain the level of skills necessary for correct reining performance.

Watching reining videos and going to shows will also help you get an idea of the maneuvers and the showing aspects of the sport. But nothing will help you get the feel for reining as much as a solid, experienced reining horse. Too many beginners make the mistake of trying to train a horse at the same time they are learning. This is fine when you are working on simple events. But reining is too complicated for you and your horse to learn at the same time. In fact, most professional trainers and coaches agree that a beginner reiner has so much to learn that he or she will probably wear out a horse learning it.

You can speed your learning process and save your horse by having a knowledgeable trainer train your horse and give you lessons on a regular basis. A trainer keeps your horse's body position and responsiveness up to par while you learn to coordinate your aids and feel the responses. This guarantees that the feels you are internalizing are the correct ones.

In addition to the aforementioned learning approaches, read all you can on the topic of reining. In this chapter, I will help you improve your reining performance by giving you a detailed description of every maneuver. I will also provide you with a clear picture of the aids you need to use to perform each maneuver at your horse's best level of ability. Since this book focuses on horsemanship rather than schooling the horse, I will focus on your part in the horse-rider equation, and assume that your horse is already schooled for reining.

Clearly, body control is important to the rider of a reining horse. Reining is the ultimate in body control. And if you are effective at all the body-control exercises described in chapter 14, you are well on your way to developing the level of feel necessary for winning reining patterns. Therefore, before we begin working on maneuvers, run a test on your horse to see how you and he team up for body-control exercises. If there is a stiff part of his body that he won't let you move and control, you will need to gain his cooperation and responsiveness before you can expect winning reining.

Knowing that you and your horse are doing well at body control, let's begin the foundation maneuver of reining: the circle.

Circles

Circles are the foundation to all reining maneuvers. A horse who does not lope and gallop correct circles cannot stop straight. His spins and rollbacks will be correct on one side but mediocre on the other. His back up will be crooked and his lead changes will suffer. This is because the circle is where the straightening of your horse begins and is maintained.

Your reining horse should lope or gallop circles on loose reins, carrying himself on the circle without your having to use your aids very much to keep him on the circle track. He should maintain the rhythm and pace at which you place him until you ask for a change.

Place your legs against your horse, make contact with his mouth, and lope circles. Give him some slack in the reins and sit quietly. Focus on how your horse feels. Is he between your reins and your legs? If he is, he does not push against either the inside rein and leg or the outside rein and leg.

If your horse feels as though he is trying to ride a smaller circle than what you are asking him to do, he is actually falling to the inside, pushing against your inside aids. If you look

This horse lopes balanced circles on loose reins. He stays between my reins and no matter where I move my rein hand, my horse's withers are directly under it. (Photo: Ted Gard)

down his neck, he is almost certainly bent the wrong way, carrying his head to the outside of the circle. Use your inside hand and inside leg to move him out on the track you want him to take.

Just as described in the discussion of guiding in chapter 14, your horse's body should be straight from poll to tail. If you can see more than the corner of your horse's inside eye, there is too much bend in his body and his shoulders are falling out of the circle. In other words, he is pushing against your outside aids. If this is the case, tighten your outside rein and press at the cinch with your outside leg to drive his shoulder in line with his poll and tail.

Now move your rein hand to the inside about two inches. Did your horse move over? He should have felt as if you picked him up by a handle on his withers and physically moved his forehand to the inside two inches. If your horse kept going in the same direction when you moved your hand to the inside, you need to reinforce your guiding aids with your outside leg and inside hand.

Keep your weight in the middle of your horse, sitting equally on both seat bones. Shifting your weight to the inside and to the outside soon causes your horse to be out of balance. He cannot guide correctly because you force him to the left and to the right.

Learn to ride circles of various sizes. Go from large circles two-hundred-feet in diameter down to fifty-foot ones and back to larger ones again. As you vary the size of your circles, focus on moving your hand as little as possible to get a response. The slightest movement of your neck-rein hand, two inches at the most, should be sufficient to guide your horse to a smaller circle. If such slight movement does not bring a response, again reinforce it with your outside leg and inside hand.

Speed Control

Reining patterns call for you and your horse to run in large, fast circles. This is easy enough. Any horse can run fast in large circles. The difficulty with correct reining is in the fact that many times, you need to bring your horse down from large, fast circles to a small, slow circle. This must be done smoothly, preferably on loose reins, with no resistance on the part of your horse. Any horse can do this, but they have to be schooled for it and ridden correctly to maintain the schooling. I am going to show you how to ride your horse through winning speed-control exercises. Your horse will slow down from a fast gallop to a western-pleasure-type lope without your ever picking up on the reins.

First, a word about the foundation necessary to speed control. Before you begin practising speed control, make sure your horse guides faultlessly on small and large circles. If you are unsure of your horse's guiding, seek professional advice. Also, be sure you are able to sit with your horse (no bouncing) and are very supple in the midsection. Speed control demands that you push your horse with your seat. If you are not clear on the seat aids, please review chapter 8.

Lope some large, slow circles on your horse. Now that your horse is warmed up, I will talk you through the speed changes. To encourage your horse into a faster lope, hold your hand on the upper part of your horse's neck, drive your horse forward with your seat, and squeeze your legs in rhythm with his galloping stride. As with all other aids, bring these aids on your horse

The aids for speed. (1) Drive the horse forward with your seat. (2) Move your rein hand up the horse's neck. (3) Squeeze your legs in rhythm with your horse's galloping stride. (Photo: Ted Gard)

slowly but firmly. Do not expect him to suddenly burst into speed. Such responses often come from fear and are uncontrolled. This is not the response you are looking for. You want your horse to accelerate progressively over several strides.

Once you have galloped four or five large, fast circles, remove the aids. In other words, sit up above your seat bones, adopt a passive seat, quit pushing with your legs, and bring your rein hand down next to his withers without making contact with his mouth. Give your horse half to three-quarters of a circle to recognize that you are not pushing any more and slow down. If he does not slow down, lift the slack and bring him to a walk for one circle. Soon your horse will be looking for an opportunity to slow down and will take it as soon as you quit pushing. Most horses eventually respond so well that you have to push them with an outside leg so that they do not stop as you remove the speeding aids.

Flying Lead Changes

The flying lead change is a natural movement your horse performs when he changes from one lope lead to the other during the moment of suspension at the lope or gallop. All reining patterns require at least one lead change in each direction. And more points can be lost for missed lead changes than for any other less-than-perfect maneuver.

Although lead changes are the phobia of many amateur reiners, you need not fear. As you worked your horse on guiding you learned to feel when he travelled straight and how to correct him when he didn't. While practicing haunches-in, you learned to move his hindquarters to the left and to the right of the line of travel while holding his shoulders up and perpendicular to the ground. The skills you acquired while mastering these two exercises will pay off in your flying-lead changes.

If your horse is athletic and guides well, you can gallop a circle to the left, neck rein him to the right, and he will probably change leads. Some reining-horse riders do it this way. This method leads to problems, however, because the lead change happens as a result of a change of direction. In other words, the horse changes direction and then changes leads. Invariably, the horse changes leads in the front, then changes behind one stride later. After several of these changes the horse begins to anticipate the change of direction and comes across the middle of the show arena leading with his outside shoulder. The horse changes direction and changes leads in the front, but the hindquarters, falling to the outside of the circle, are never in a position to change leads. The straight body position essential to the flying lead change is lost and so is the lead change.

I will show you how to coordinate your aids to change leads on a straight line. You can practice this type of lead change as much as you want and, if you do things correctly, your horse will only get better at it. This type of lead change allows you to change leads and then change direction, thereby eliminating the problem with anticipation and loss of position. It allows for a hind leg and front leg lead change during the same moment of suspension. And it ensures hind lead change by moving the hindquarters in the direction of the change before the horse gets any indication that you may change direction. In fact, most of the time you do not change direction, but rather continue in a straight line. The theory is based on the

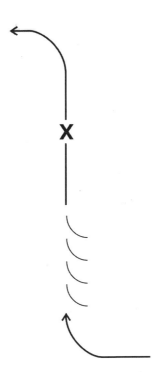

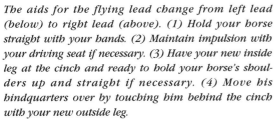

The aids for the flying lead change from left lead (below) to right lead (above). (1) Hold your horse straight with your hands. (2) Maintain impulsion with your driving seat if necessary. (3) Have your new inside leg at the cinch and ready to hold your horse's shoulders up and straight if necessary. (4) Move his hindquarters over by touching him behind the cinch with your new outside leg.

To reaffirm leg aids and flying lead changes, lope around the riding surface, turn on the center line, and ask for haunches-in. Once your horse has responded to your haunches-in aids, let him straighten out for a few strides, then ask for a flying lead change at X. Continue to ride straight, then turn in the new direction.

fact that your horse has learned, through haunches-in, to move his hindquarters away from your displacing leg while his shoulders remain upright and in a straight line.

Now lope your horse in a straight line on the left lead and I will talk you through a flying lead change.

Because it is important that the horse's forehand be elevated, establish contact with the horse's mouth and drive gently with your seat. Your horse's back will round up under the saddle and he will bring his hind legs deeper under himself. Keep your upper body upright and steady, your weight equally divided above both seat bones, and your midsection loose and actively driving your horse. As you keep your horse collected and straight by light contact on his mouth, move your left leg back on his rib cage and press his hindquarters over, as in a haunches-in.

Your horse's conditioned response is to move his hindquarters away from your leg. He cannot do so, however, while on the left lead and pushing with his left hind leg. In order to respond, he changes leads and begins to push himself with the right hind leg. Voila! You have a flying lead change! Take your leg away, let the reins go loose, and continue in a straight line. Remember, no change of direction. For a change from right-to-left, simply move your right leg back as you hold your horse straight and collected.

Your horse might not respond to the lead change cues for two reasons. The first is that you were not successful in holding his shoulders upright and his body straight. This can be relatively difficult, particularly on older horses who have been travelling crooked and have never learned to guide correctly. You can easily identify which shoulder your horse is falling onto. He typically feels heavier on your hand on that side and finds it difficult to change leads to that same side. If your horse feels heavier or dull on your right hand, for example, it is because he carries more weight on his right shoulder than on any of his other limbs. He will tend to fall into the circles to the right and even lope circles with his nose to the outside. He will lope straight lines bent to the left. He will miss many hind-leg lead changes from left to right because his right shoulder is leading the right hind leg.

Correct him by picking up on your right rein and pressing his shoulders over to the left with your right leg as you keep him loping straight. Hold the corrective aids for a few strides, then release. As soon as he falls to the right, pick him up and correct him again.

The other reason your horse may not have changed leads could be that he is not responsive enough to the displacing leg. If you suspect that this is the case, forget about the lead change. Softly transition down to a jog and remind your horse of the desired response by performing a haunches-in in the direction of the lead change. Then pick up a lope and try again.

To anchor your horse's response to your flying lead change aids, practice lead changes on the circles. Lope circles to the right on the right lead. Ride your horse on the bit and forward. While remaining on the circle, apply your lead change aids and keep riding your horse forward, asking him to change from a right lead to a left lead while loping circles to the right. Once your horse changes to counter canter, keep your inside leg on him to indicate that you expect him to continue loping even if it is not comfortable. After a few circles, move your inside leg to the front cinch, effect a displacing leg with your outside leg, and ask for a flying lead change from counter canter to the correct lead.

Avoid spurring or whipping a horse into a lead change. Horses are easily frightened at the lope and you will soon find yourself with a runaway horse—and for good reason.

Spins

The spin is a 360-degree turn the horse performs around his hindquarters. The spin should be flat—in other words, the horse should not bounce up and down as he goes around but rather stay level as his front legs take trot-like steps.

In a spin to the left, the horse begins by reaching left with his left front leg. Then he reaches in front of it with his right front before reaching left with the inside left leg again, and so on. The inside hind leg, in this case the left hind, should remain in place as the pivot foot or move no more than 10 or 12 inches. The horse's poll should be either level with or slightly higher than his withers. His head may be held naturally or slightly flexed at the poll. His body should be straight or have very little bend in the direction of the spin—no more than in the circles. In a fast spin, the horse draws his inside hind leg deep under himself and rounds his back under the saddle. This shift of weight over his inside hind leg makes it possible for him to move his front legs faster.

Although they vary slightly, depending on your horse's level of accomplishment in the maneuver, the aids for the spin are essentially the same as the guiding aids. Ride with two hands until you are very familiar with the aids

This picture and the next two show the sequence of movement during the spin. In this picture, the horse begins the spin to the left by reaching sideways and to the left with his left front leg. He balances himself on his inside hind leg as he lifts his right hind to set it down again as he pivots. Note the rider's low hand position and the loose reins as the horse begins the turn. (Photo: Ted Gard)

The horse has crossed his front legs and prepares to transfer weight to his outside front leg in order to reach left with the inside leg again. (Photo: Ted Gard)

The horse prepares to cross his outside front leg ahead of the inside front for another step of the spin. His back is round, his croup lowered, and his inside hind leg deep under his body. Your horse should spin on loose reins. Avoid the common mistake of pulling your horse around into a spin. The more contact you make with his mouth, the less he spins. (Photo: Ted Gard)

and the feel of the correct response. If you plan to show your horse during this stage, try to enter classes that allow two-handed riding.

Let's begin at the walk. Ride your horse in a circle twelve feet in diameter. Keep his walk very forward and his body straight. Even though he is not yet in a spin, walking this small circle with his body straight forces your horse to step across with his front legs and prepares him for the maneuver.

Sit evenly on your seat bones and be sure your upper body is straight. Leaning to the inside or the outside are the most common problems amateur reiners face. Either way puts your horse out of balance, forcing him to move his pivot foot, hollow his back, or overbend his body to keep you above his center of gravity. Leaning forward places your weight over your horse's shoulders and forces him to take short steps forward with his front legs rather than stepping to the side.

Still walking that twelve-foot circle, lift both hands about four inches away from their low position close to your horse's withers and into the direction of the spin. Be sure your outside rein touches your horse's neck, but do not let

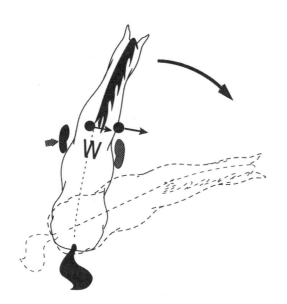

The aids for the spin. (1) Move both hands in the direction of the spin. (2) Reinforce your rein aids with your outside leg if necessary. (3) Keep your seat centered on the horse, not leaning one way or the other.

your neck-rein hand cross the center of his neck. There should be no contact with your horse's mouth yet and your outside leg should remain passive. This is the lightest form of spin aids.

Your horse should spin in response to the light aids. If he does not respond, reinforce the neck rein by making contact with the inside rein and pressing at the cinch with the outside leg or spur. When your horse goes into the spin, immediately remove the reinforcing aids and let him turn on the light neck-rein cue. Avoid pulling on your horse while he is turning around. Doing so forces your horse to brace against your aids, elevate too much in the forehand, and eventually back up into the turn. Let him turn freely on loose rein. Focus on staying centered and light handed.

To stop your horse from turning, say "whoa" and lift the slack from the reins.

Always give your horse approximately three seconds to respond to the light neck-rein cue before reinforcing it with your other aids. This ensures that your horse has time to feel and learn to respond to the light neck rein. Eventually, a small vibration of the rein will suffice to send him into a spin.

Feel for the rhythmic step...step...step...step of your horse's front legs in the spin. If your horse feels like step.......step..step...step ....step, his rhythm is poor. It may be because you spin him fast too often or spin him

too fast for his level of schooling and ability. Either way, slow down and be sure your horse is straight and supple. Refrain from adding speed to the spins until your horse spins with rhythm on a light neck rein.

To add speed to the spins, apply the same light neck rein and cluck to your horse. He if speeds up, spin one more turn and stop. If he does not speed up in response to the cluck, bump him with your outside leg or spur. Always reward him for speeding up by spinning as little as one-half or three-quarters of a spin, then riding him out of it or stopping him. Fast spins are very demanding for a horse and too many of them can soon cause your horse to quit trying every time you ask.

Learn to count the number of spins your horse has executed by saying the count upon completion of each spin. If a pattern calls for three spins, for example, say "one" as your horse completes the first spin, "two" as he completes the second one, and "whoa" when he completes the third. If your horse spins very fast, be sure to say "whoa" before the end of the last spin so that he will have time to react and stop before overspinning. Overspinning is considered a fault and incurs penalty points.

Showing always increases the anxiety level and, as a result, many amateur reiners do not get their horse's spins shown. They get in a hurry and end up pulling on their horses and scaring them. Take your time when you get into the show ring. If your horse seems to take forever to start into the spin, he probably is doing just fine. You've learned to ride him correctly at home; let him show you and the judge what he can do at the show.

Back up

The back up, like all other maneuvers, is an indication of how much control and cooperation you have with your horse. Every reining pattern calls for a back up maneuver.

In a correct back up, your horse responds to relatively loose reins as he flexes at the poll, rounds his back, lowers his croup, and elevates his withers. He backs up straight without tossing his head or opening his mouth.

To back your horse, slowly lift the slack out of the reins and squeeze the calves of your legs against his sides. If your horse backs crooked to the right, effect a right displacing leg and press his hindquarters over and in line with the rest of his body. At the same time, press his shoulders over to the left with your left leg at the cinch.

If your horse freezes in the back up, you probably are pulling on him with your hands. Lighten up the hands and place more emphasis on your leg aids to motivate him into movement.

To speed up the maneuver, increase your leg aids by using reinforcing legs. For more speed, press with the lower legs and spurs immediately behind the cinch. Avoid increasing the contact on your horse's mouth. Increased contact forces him to brace against your hands. As a result, stiffness occurs in the shoulders and back, hindering his ability to move his limbs at a faster pace.

The back up is very closely related to the stop. In fact, backing up a few steps is often required as a correction for a poor stop. For this reason it is important that you not pull, jerk, or seesaw on your horse's mouth when backing up. The resultant injuries, fear, and resistance would surely show up in the stops, seriously compromising the future of your winning reining horse.

Rollbacks

The rollback is a 180-degree turn during which the horse's front feet leave the ground while all of his weight is transferred onto his hindquarters. The horse comes out of the turn at the lope. The turn must be quick but the horse must lope off quietly. The path of exit from the rollback must be the same as the path of entry. In other words, the horse's front feet must be off the ground throughout the turn.

Correct rollbacks are possible only if your horse's back is round and his hind legs are deep under his body. In the early stages, you may want to bend his body slightly in the direction of the turn. Very soon, however, you will need to let him do the rollback with his body straight. Otherwise, you will have problems when the time comes to roll back with only one hand on the reins, as is required in the show ring. Allow your horse to carry his head in a natural position because too much flexion at the poll hinders your horse's ability to balance himself during this maneuver.

The key to a smooth, crisp, correct rollback is to expect the horse to lope out of the turn entirely on his own. It is not speed that causes a horse to execute a fast rollback; rather, it is the anticipation of loping off in the opposite direction. My method of coordinating the aids for rollback results in crisp turns and soft, balanced lope off. Here is how it works for a rollback to the left (for a rollback to the right, simply reverse the aids).

Although horse show rollbacks are done from a sliding stop, we will begin our rollback lesson from the back up. This allows you to get the feel of the rollback aids and horse without developing stiffness and crookedness in the stop.

Walk your horse forward, then stop. Ask for a straight, medium-speed back up. Be sure to stay light and soft with your hands. Three or four steps into the back up, and while your horse is still in the process of backing up, lift both hands toward your left shoulder. Lift your hands about ten or twelve inches higher than the normal hand position close to your horse's withers. (This is an important difference between the spin aids and the rollback aids. In the spin, you encourage your horse to remain flat. In the rollback, you encourage him to lift.) Your left hand should be three or four inches higher than your right hand, just enough to tip your horse's neck to the left. Your weight should remain evenly distributed over your seat bones.

Your horse shifts his weight on his hind legs and sweeps around in response to your rein. Two-thirds of the way through the turn, move your hands forward to release the reins and let him out of the turn. At the same time, press your right leg behind the cinch to ensure a lope departure without trotting strides. Your horse lopes off in a smooth, controlled manner.

This and the next two photographs show the sequence of movement during a rollback. Immediately after the stop, the horse pushes his front quarters off the ground and begins a rotation over his deeply engaged hindquarters. (Photo: Ted Gard)

Pushing with his outside hind leg, the horse lopes off out of the turn as his front legs touches the ground. (Photo: Ted Gard)

Without his front legs touching the ground, the horse continues his rotation. This horse is two-thirds of the way through the rollback. It is at this point of the turn that the rider presses his outside leg against the horse to ensure that he will lope out of the turn. (Photo: Ted Gard)

In the early stages of rollbacks, use two hands to help maintain correct positioning. Lift your outside hand approximately twelve inches above the withers. Lift your inside hand slightly higher to help your horse hold his inside shoulder up. This rider's hands are positioned for a rollback to the right. (Photo: Ted Gard)

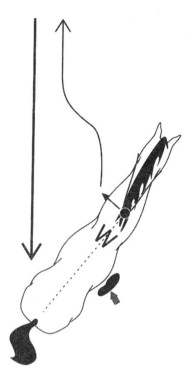

The aids for the finished rollback. (1) Lift your rein hand in the direction of your shoulder. (2) Two-thirds of the way through the turn, press with your outside leg behind the cinch as you move your hand forward to give him slack. (3) Be sure your weight remains centered on your horse.

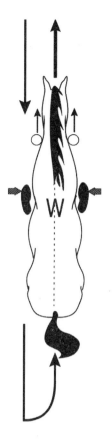

The aids for correcting the lazy rollback. Once your horse is turned in the new direction, release the reins and bump him on the forearms simultaneously with both legs. The two reinforcing legs will bring him to lope and build his anticipation for lope departure after a rollback.

Now let's look at why your horse may not have responded and what you can do about it. The following questions and answers should be helpful:

1. Did your horse put his head up and refuse to budge when you lifted your hands? Go back to body-control exercises and supple his stiff body parts.

2. Did he remain soft to your hands but not move his forehand? Bump him with a reinforcing leg at the shoulder or press your spur at the cinch the next time you ask for a rollback.

3. Did he turn, but in a somewhat sluggish manner, feel lazy to your leg, and trot out of the rollback? For the next three or four rollbacks, hurry him out of the turn by bumping him hard on the shoulders with simultaneous reinforcing legs after he has finished the rollback. Be

sure not to bump him while he is in the turn, no matter how slow he is at turning. What you are doing is building in his mind the anticipation of hurrying out of the turn. This anticipation will cause him to hurry through the turn. Be careful not to overdo this correction. Bump him out of a half dozen turns, then try him again without the reinforcing legs. Soon, all you will have to do to get a crisp turn followed by a smooth, balanced lope will be stop your horse and lift your hand in the direction of your shoulder.

Avoid making many rollbacks from sliding stops. Your horse will begin to anticipate the turns and, as a result, will stop crooked.

The reining rules state that a horse may come out of the rollback on either lead as long as he is on the correct lead by the time he turns at the end of the arena. However, there is no reason for your horse to be on the wrong lead if he responds to your rein, your seat remains over his center of gravity, and your outside leg presses against his side at the correct moment.

The rollback combines three maneuvers in a short second: the stop, turn, and lope departure. It requires feel and timing. Focus on soft aids and sharp response as you practice it at slow speed.

Sliding Stops

The sliding stop is potentially the most spectacular maneuver in equine sport. The sight of a wide-open galloping horse coming to a stop in a seemingly effortless meltdown is topped only by the thrill of riding one. The reining horse lopes down one side of the arena, balanced, on loose reins. As he rounds the end of the riding space the horse begins to gain incremental speed with every stride. As he reaches the middle of the arena, the horse is galloping almost full-out. His neck is stretched ahead. His hind legs reach deep under his body. He is still gaining speed. Then, as if by magic, the picture changes. The horse's hindquarters seem to disappear in a cloud of dust. His front legs are "paddling" in a balanced rhythm. His back is round to the point that the saddle skirting is raised about six inches above his loin. His hind feet are so deep under him they are even with the front cinch of the saddle.

He has come to a standstill. Standing relaxed, his head level with his withers and ears pointed

forward, he is nevertheless at attention, Amazingly enough, the rider seemed to have done nothing throughout the maneuver. The reins were just as loose through the stop as they were when the horse was loping. There was no spurring or jabbing or whipping as the horse was accelerating. And there was no sudden upper-body movement as the horse melted into the ground and came to a standstill. It was as close to perfect as horsemanship and horse power can make a maneuver. It was a sliding stop.

This lesson on sliding stops is organized in four parts. First, I talk about good reining ground. Then I show you how to coordinate your aids for the basic sliding stop from the fast lope. Then I discuss what to do if your horse does not respond to your aids as he should. I finish the discussion on reining with tips on how to ride an important component of the winning sliding stop: the rundown.

Good reining ground is paramount to a sliding stop. So important, in fact, that most reining-horse exhibitors will not haul to a show, or once there will not show their reining horses, if the ground is not as it should be.

Author slides Olds Little Okie to a stop in NRHA Open reining. The rider sits in balance. A subtle push in the stirrups and a straight yet supple back, combined with a well-schooled horse, allow him to remain deep in the saddle in spite of the hard run and stop. (Photo: Sharon Latimer)

Although very deep into the ground, this horse is relaxed and confident as evidenced by the trotting motion of his front legs. His back is round and he slides to a stop on very light bit pressure. (Photo: Sharon Latimer)

Reining ground is composed of two essential parts: the base and the surface. The base must be sufficiently hard to prevent the horse's hind toes from digging into the heavy dirt during the slide. A twelve-hundred-pound horse and rider team sliding at thirty miles per hour can break a horse's phalanx if the horse's toe were to dig into the dirt and flip the foot and pastern over itself. At best, the horse feels tremendous pain from the strain on his ligaments and eventually begins to brace himself with his front legs or even quits stopping. The base must be level. It can be composed of hard-packed clay, stone dust, or a mixture of any type of soil that will pack under the horse's feet.

The surface must allow for sufficient cushioning without being so heavy as to diminish the length of the sliding stop. It should be no deeper than three inches. The best materials for reining surfaces are masonry sand, naturally washed sand, such as river sand, or industrially washed sand. These materials also form an ideal riding surface for a host of other equine sports because the organic elements have been washed out of the sand, leaving pure rock, which does not pack and releases very little dust.

Keep the surface loose and level by working the sand on a regular basis. This is called dragging the ground. If you ride more than three horses a day on the surface, you will need to drag on a daily basis; otherwise, every second or third day is sufficient. Be sure to use a sufficiently light implement, and one that is built so that it will ride on top of the base and not dig into it. Digging up the base and mixing it with the surface material will cause the surface to pack hard, compromising both the base and the surface.

Now, let's talk about coordinating your aids for the sliding stop. Put your reining horse at the lope and ride several large, slow circles. Ride him out of the circle on some straight lines. Check that he guides well and goes on the bit when you ask.

Now go back to the large circles and increase the tempo to a fast lope. Lope several more circles, until your horse feels as though he wants

Through her deep yet relaxed stop this horse shows the ultimate result of suppling and body control. The loose reins are proof that pulling on the reins is not necessary for stopping. Rather, subtle seat aids and soft asking hands bring the best results. Think of your aids as saying, "Stop, please." (Photo: Sharon Latimer)

to slow down and stop. When you feel he is looking for a break, keep your upper body straight, effect a passive seat, push on your stirrups with the balls of your feet, say "whoooooa" slowly and—halfway through saying the word—slowly lift the slack out of the reins. Be sure you are not pushing him with your legs. If your horse is wearing sliding plates and you are riding on good reining ground, he should have slid five to ten feet. As you stand still and reward him for a nice effort, I'll tell you why I asked you to apply your aids this way.

Leaning your upper body forward or backward as you prepare to stop your horse changes his balance and hinders his ability to stop correctly. Nothing in your upper body should change immediately before a stop. Also key to a correct sliding stop is saying "whoa" slowly. The long, dragged-out version of the word gives your horse time to react to your wish before you make contact with his mouth. The long "whoooooa" also places your body in slow mode rather than the quick reflexes you foster when you say a short "whoa." This slow mode is key to the next aid you applied—lifting the slack out of the reins very slowly until you feel your horse's mouth. If your body is in quick mode, your hand moves fast and your horse does not have time to prepare himself for the stop. But since you spoke slowly to your horse and moved your hand slowly to make contact with his mouth, he had time to prepare for the stop. It takes time for the horse to quit pushing himself forward, round his back, lower his croup, and bring his hind legs deep under himself in preparation for a slide. If you give him the time to get ready, your horse will stop in a relaxed and balanced manner and, with speed, will slide more than thirty feet. If you are quick with your aids, pulling or jerking on his mouth, he will associate the stopping aids with pain and will begin to stop on his forehand to avoid it.

What if you did everything right and your horse did not give you that nice effort? There may be several reasons. He may be stiff, rather than supple and straight in his body. If this is the case, you will not be able to perform correctly every body-control exercise described in chapter 14. Take some time away from the stops and fix the foundation.

Your horse may be out of condition and his soft muscles may not be strong enough to hold a sliding stop. Generally speaking, if your horse is overweight and has a "hay belly," his muscles are too soft for him to stop correctly. Be sure to get him fit before asking for big stops.

Or your horse may simply need a reminder that "whoooooa" means what it says. Now I will show you how to reprimand your horse without frightening him and losing correctness in your stops.

If your horse stopped in a lazy manner, dribbling down to a trot and then stopping, or if he began the stop correctly but walked out of it at the end, you need to instill some respect for the light contact you made with his mouth. The next time he stops this way, hold the light contact you established in the stop and back him up one or two steps by bumping him on the shoulders with alternating reinforcing legs immediately after the stop. Do not pull harder on his mouth. You want him to stop on light contact so that he can be relaxed and balanced. Two

steps of back up is sufficient. Any more than this and it becomes a back up exercise.

If your horse stopped hard but felt stiff and bouncy in the forehand (you can feel this through your thighs), you need to take some of the stiffness and fear out and show him that he can relax his shoulders. The next time he stops this way, hold the light contact you established during the stop, place you legs against your horse, and drive him forward out of the stop immediately after the stop. In other words, the stop and driving forward on the bit becomes one continuous maneuver. Your horse learns to relax and move his shoulders through the sliding stop instead of bracing against your hands. Since you will reward your horse by letting him stand still as soon as he relaxes again, you need not worry about taking the stop out of your horse by riding him forward.

Once you and your horse can slide four to eight feet correctly, all you need to slide twenty-five to thirty feet is more speed. You will gain this necessary speed during the rundown.

Lope your horse on a large oval similar to a race track. Lean your shoulders behind your hips about one inch and push your stirrups forward, slightly ahead of the cinch. Place your hand down on your horse's withers and make sure that there is slack in the reins. This body position not only enables you to ride a long slide softly and correctly, but also eventually becomes a cue for your horse to run hard.

If your horse gained speed, let him gallop for two or three hundred yards. Now sit up, bring your legs under your seat bones, and let him slow down. If he did not gain speed, encourage him by bumping him with reinforcing legs on his elbows. Be sure you encourage progressive speed gain rather than sudden bursts. The progressive gain of speed all the way into the stop is fundamental to the long slide. When you are comfortable with the speed at which your horse is travelling, apply the stopping aids you learned at the lope and see how far you slide.

Be sure you go about this in a progressive manner. If you run your horse hard every time you ride him or each time you guide him on a straight line, you will soon find yourself on a runaway horse. Professional reiners ride their horses hard one day a week and spend the other schooling sessions keeping them correct and relaxed. Nowhere is this more important than in the rundowns.

Stopping and sliding is first and foremost a mind-set. You must make your horse mentally ready to stop, then let him stop. Do it and you will be rewarded with an exceptional feeling of achievement.

CHAPTER 17

Barrel Racing and Pole Bending

Run hard, slow down, turn, guide, and change leads; all in less than twenty seconds.

Speed events are some of the most popular and entertaining sports in which you can involve yourself and your horse. Running them correctly demands a great deal of horsemanship. A great many things happen fast while you run a barrel-racing or a pole-bending pattern. Although barrel racing and pole bending appear quite simple, in the course of a run your barrel-racing or pole-bending horse has to propel himself at great speed at least three times. He has to round his back and engage his hindquarters deep under himself at least three times. He must execute flying lead changes, at least once in the case of a barrel horse, ten times in the case of a pole-bending horse. He has to hold his shoulders up in the turns and he has to guide extremely well at very high speeds. Not so simple when it all happens in less than twenty seconds.

Your horse has a tough job, but yours is just as demanding: stay out of his way most of the time and help him along the rest of the time.

In this chapter, I will talk you through a barrel race and a pole-bending race and detail the aids you need to use to ensure as fast a run as your horse can possibly deliver. To help you with the timing of your aids, I will divide the barrel and pole turn into three parts: the pocket, the back side of the turn, and the final section of the turn.

Barrel Racing

The race begins in the alley leading into the show arena. You have already warmed up your horse by trotting and loping circles and straight lines. You

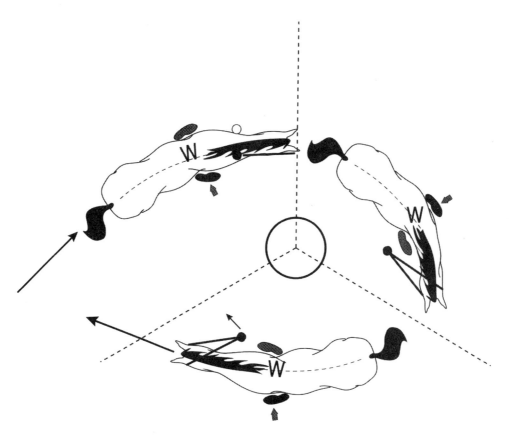

The aids during a turn around the barrel. In the first part of the turn, press your inside leg at the cinch and your inside rein against your horse's neck to hold his shoulder up and guide him in the pocket. In the second part of the turn, place your outside leg against your horse to keep him forward and help him hold his hindquarters so that they do not swing out. Guide him with a combination neck/opening rein. In the final section of the turn, continue to guide your horse with a combination neck/opening rein as you place your outside leg at the cinch to bring his shoulders in line with the path to the next barrel.

checked his responsiveness by doing haunches-in and lateral bending exercises, such as shoulder-up. You warmed up his back and hindquarter muscles through stops and back ups. You reinforced his response to the outside guiding rein through spins and rollbacks. The rodeo announcer has called your name. You are ready to go.

Your horse gallops in a straight line to a pocket about ten feet from the first barrel and slightly to the left of it. You guide him with both hands on the reins as you look at the area around the barrel. Bending at the hips, you lean forward with your upper body to remain in balance with your running horse.

As you get to the pocket (ten feet from the barrel) you want your horse to round his back, bring his hind feet deep under himself, and prepare for the turn by bending laterally to the right. To help him in this preparation, bring your shoulders back above your hips. As you bring your upper body into balance with his, let go of the rein with your outside hand and hold the saddle horn, keeping your elbow close to your outside hip and pushing on the horn to help you stay in balance with your horse.

Holding the rein with your inside hand, you are beginning the first of three parts in the barrel turn. Your objective in this part of the turn is to make sure your horse does not fall into the barrel but rather runs a pocket in preparation for exiting the turn. To this end, effect a right direct rein, with the rein tight against your horse's neck, and press your inside leg against your horse. These aids also ensure that your horse's shoulders stay up and you do not incur a penalty for knocking down the barrel.

This rider demonstrates the position of the outside arm as her horse enters the pocket and turns the barrel. With her elbow close to her hip, she pushes on the saddle horn as her horse approaches the barrel, which helps her remain above her horse's center of gravity as he prepares to turn. (Photo: Ted Gard)

This is the correct amount of bend while turning the barrel. Note that the bend is not only in the horse's neck but also through his torso as a result of the rider applying contact with her inside leg. (Photo: Ted Gard)

Guiding with both hands between barrels is an effective way to ensure that your horse will approach the next barrel at the correct angle for a pocket. (Photo: Ted Gard)

Too much bend in the neck forces this horse's shoulder to fall out of the turn. This incorrect position results in a loss of control in the turns, wide turns, and a costly loss of time. (Photo: Ted Gard)

Bending at the hips, pulling on the horn, and giving your horse plenty of slack in the reins are important as he leaves the turn and accelerates toward the next barrel. (Photo: Ted Gard)

This rider demonstrates the position of the inside hand during the second part of the turn. Low and to the inside of the turn, it effects a combination neck rein/opening rein. The rider's shoulders are square with those of her horse. (Photo: Ted Gard)

Exiting the turn, both rider and horse are looking at the next barrel. Precious fractions of seconds can be lost if you are late looking at the spot to which you want to ride your horse for the next barrel pocket. Such delay in focusing on the spot may translate into late application of your guiding aids and a wider, and consequently slower, turn. (Photo: Ted Gard)

Your horse is now turning the back side of the barrel, the second part of the turn. Your aids here depend on how your horse feels through the turn. If he is close to the barrel but not bumping your knee into it, and feels as though he is following his shoulders around the barrel and pushing with his hind legs, all is well. Sit upright, not leaning to the inside or the outside. Placing your outside leg against him to keep him forward and to keep his hindquarters from falling out of the turn, guide him into the turn with a combination of opening rein and neck rein. If your horse feels as though he is headed away from the barrel and making a wider turn than necessary, press your outside leg at the cinch and guide him firmly to the turn with your rein combination. (If your horse shows any inclination to run wide around the barrels, go back to walking, trotting, and loping barrels to reestablish control. If a horse does not respond to the aids at the lope, he likely will not even be aware of them at the run.)

Your horse has turned the back of the barrel and is entering the third and final section of the turn. Your goal is to position him for a tight finish to the turn and a straight line to the pocket of the second barrel. Still pushing on the horn and guiding with your inside hand, press your outside leg at the cinch and continue the opening rein/neck rein combination. Keep your eyes focused on the next barrel's pocket and rein your horse toward it. As your horse clears the barrel and begins to gain speed, lean forward from the hips and pull on the saddle horn to stay with him as his powerful hindquarters propel both of you on. Push your rein hand forward up his neck to give him plenty of slack in the reins, making it possible for him to stretch his neck for balance as he gains speed. As soon as he has regained full speed, let go of the saddle horn and again guide him with two hands in a straight line to the next pocket.

Be sure your seat stays in the saddle as you lean forward. If you lift your seat out of the saddle as you lean forward, your buttocks will hit the top of the cantle as your horse pushes out of the turn. Consequently, you will find yourself behind your horse's center of gravity and probably pulling on the reins in an effort to recapture your seat.

Speed, balance, and anticipation will take care of the flying lead change between the first and second barrels. To turn the second and third barrels, simply reverse the aids described for the first barrel.

Learn to coordinate your aids at the walk and trot. When you are secure in their application, go on to the lope. Eventually, running the cloverleaf pattern will be barrels of fun.

Pole Bending

Pole bending is also a timed event that demands a great deal of horsemanship on your part and tremendous athletic ability on your horse's part. Some portions of the pole-bending pattern are very similar to barrel racing. In the rundown as well as in the turn around the end poles, use your aids in the same way you do when running between barrels and turning a barrel. Pole bending differs most from barrel racing when you are running between the poles. In the rest of this chapter, I will talk you through running between the poles.

Let's say that you have run down to the end of the poles, turned the far pole, and are just beginning to run between the poles.

Assuming that your turn around the first pole was to the left, your first change of direction is to the right. Prepare your horse for the change of direction and the change of leads as his head clears the first pole. Press your inside leg (in this case, your right leg) at the cinch to help your

The aids for running up the poles. (1) Press your right leg at the cinch to hold your horse's shoulders up in the turn. (2) Effect a displacing left leg to bend your horse around the pole and support him for the flying lead change. (3) Guide your horse through the poles with both hands on the reins. (4) Using a direct rein, bend him slightly in the direction of the turn.

horse hold his shoulders up in the turn. Effect a displacing leg with your outside (left) leg, to help your horse bend slightly in the direction of the turn and hold his hindquarters in place for a lead change. Guide your horse through the poles with both hands on the reins. Using a direct rein, bend him slightly in the direction of the turn as you apply your leg aids.

Your horse should change leads and turn before he gets to the second pole. Once his head clears this pole, apply the aids for the next turn, and so on. Continue up the poles, turning the last one the same way you turned barrels. Then gallop down the poles again until you turn the last one. Then, having turned the last pole, bend forward from the hips and run home to the money!

CHAPTER 18

Cutting

It's better to cut a bad cow good than a good cow bad.

Riding a cutting horse is one of the most exhilarating experiences of the equestrian world. On very loose reins, and totally on his own, the cutting horse explodes in front of the cow. He gets low to the ground, legs spread wide, ears forward. His hind feet are deep under him as he sweeps over them and cuts the cow off to the right. For a fraction of a second, the cow looks as though she is going to turn to her right and run. The horse sweeps to his left. The cow stops. The horse lands halfway through the turn, one front leg cocked and ready to respond to the next clue the cow gives him.

Cutting has its origins in the sorting out of cattle on the ranches of the Old West. Nowadays, it is a sophisticated equestrian event that features some of the richest purses available to any horse and rider team.

In a cutting competition, you have two and one-half minutes to cut a minimum of two cows out of a herd and show the judge how athletic and cow-smart your horse is. The well-known quotation at the beginning of this chapter states—in very few words—the way to a winning cutting performance: Regardless of the cattle, the ground, or anything else, if you ride well you will be successful. To show your horse to the best of his ability, you have to be able to sit correctly and in balance through the hard stops and fast turns. In this chapter, I will explain how to sit the cutting horse and how to use your hands and legs while cutting a cow.

Elaine Speight, aboard the eight-year-old gelding Hot Bar Con, shows the form that led her to the Reserve Championship title of the Non-Pro Division at the 1992 International Cutting Competition in Houston, Texas. Her body is upright and balanced, her shoulders are square with her horse's shoulders, and her head follows the movements of the cow. (Photo: Don Shugart)

Your Head and Upper Body

Your head must follow the cow at all times. In fact, it is the only part of your anatomy that moves with the cow. The rest of your body moves with your horse.

With your eyes on the cow, read her body language and anticipate the next move your horse will have to make to retain his working advantage. By matching the signals the cow gives you with your horse's position, you can determine whether he needs help or not. Avoid looking down at your horse. If you take your eyes away from the cow for a second, your horse may find himself out of his working position and you will be unaware that he needed help. The result may be a lost cow and a low score.

Your upper body should remain upright at all times, with your shoulders square with your horse's shoulders.

Twisting the upper body into the turn or to look at the cow causes your legs to move against your horse and may confuse him. Leaning back before a stop changes your center

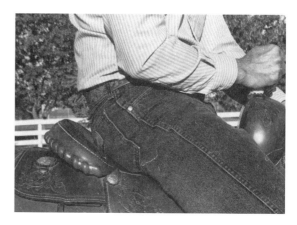

Sit in the middle of the saddle, leaving sufficient space between your seat and the cantle (about the width of your hand). This prevents the cantle from launching you forward as your horse pushes hard out of a turn.

The correct upper body position riding into a hard stop: a slight rounding of the lower back. Also pictured, the rider sitting too close to the cantle.

Falling over the horn is often the result of being too stiff in the midsection and consequently unable to absorb the quick movements of the horse.

of gravity and momentarily puts your horse off balance. Leaning left or right pulls your horse down into a turn or out of a turn and may cause him to lose a cow. At best, it will cause your horse to perform what are commonly called barrel turns (small circle turns), rather than a hard stop followed by an immediate turn over the hocks.

Your Seat

Cutting horses stop hard, turn hard, and leave fast—all within a fraction of a second. The challenge to you is to remain in balance with the horse, as these maneuvers happen very suddenly. The flat, long seat of the cutting saddle is designed to help you achieve that goal. The long seat permits you to slide back and forth as the horse stops and turns. Its flat design allows you to be close to the horse at all times, no matter where you are in the saddle. To draw maximum benefits from the cutting saddle and remain in balance through these hard turns, sit in the middle of the saddle. Leaving plenty of space between the cantle and your seat, as well as between the swells and your seat, ensures that you will not be thrown forward as your horse pushes off hard.

For slow work and periods of loping in front of the cow, sit upright on your seat bones, in the basic position (refer to chapt. 4). When the cow indicates that she is going to stop, round your lower back and tuck your jeans pockets under yourself. This tilting backward of your pelvis absorbs some of the momentum of the stop and lets you stay in balance with your horse.

As with all types of riding, keep your buttocks and thigh muscles relaxed. Gripping to stay on the cutting horse has the same results as on any other well-tuned equine athlete—it destroys performance.

Your Legs

In spite of the impression that the cutting horse does all his work on his own, successful cutting-horse riders use one or both legs frequently and in various combinations when working a cow.

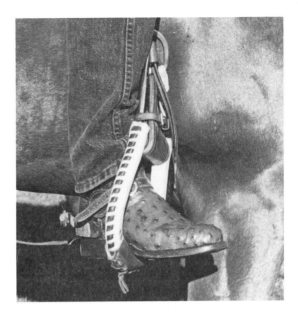

Cutters use oxbow stirrups and wear them deep to guard against a loss of stirrup during a hard ride.

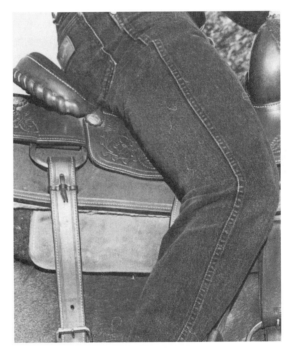

Gripping with the thighs leads to a loss of balance as your legs fall back. You may also accidentally spur your horse out of position.

To be effective, your legs must be at the right place on your horse's side. The leg and foot position described in chapter 4 is very effective when riding a cutting horse.

Now to explain how to use your legs. Imagine that you are riding a cutting horse. He is loping across the pen, his head even with the cow's shoulder. He is rating the cow and maintaining his position.

The cow stops and turns. Your horse stops and turns and is again parallel with the cow.

Except this time, your horse's head is even with the cow's hip and he is losing his working advantage. He is in danger of falling behind the cow and losing the cow to the herd. In this situation, press both legs against your horse as you drive him with your seat to urge him into position.

Your horse regains his position and heads the cow in the other direction. His stop is clean but you know he never quite finishes his turns to the left. Instead of turning a full 180 degrees as he should, he usually turns about 100 degrees and lopes off in the direction of the cow. This incomplete turn results in a loss of working advantage and, eventually, the loss of the cow. Press your right leg at the cinch to help your horse finish his turn and maintain his working advantage over the cow.

Pushing your feet forward can become a cue for your horse to stop and back up. Note the somewhat loose back cinch, which lets the horse use his back and get deep in the ground without pulling the saddle tree into his back and causing soreness.

Now your horse is loping across the pen with the cow on his right. Although he is rating the cow well, he feels as though he is leaning in the direction of the cow. Unless you help him and correct his line of travel, he will get too close to the cow and again lose his working advantage. Press your right leg (the one closest to the cow) at the cinch and encourage him to put some distance between his body and that of the cow.

If your horse tends to fall away from the cow as he lopes across the pen, however, press with your herd leg (the leg closer to the herd) and realign his direction so that he maintains ground to the cow.

Your Hands and the Saddle Horn

When riding with one hand on the reins, your rein hand should be low on your horse's neck, immediately in front of the saddle pad. It should stay in this position during the entire cut and until you are ready to quit the cow. Raising the rein during cutting competition may be considered a rein cue and result in penalty points.

When riding with two hands, as during schooling, keep your hands low as you make contact with your horse's mouth. Your cutting horse must be confident in lowering his head and working eye-to-eye with the cow. Lifting your hands above the swells will eventually lead him to work with his head carried high and cause problems in stops and turns.

Once your horse begins to make some hard moves, you will benefit from using the saddle horn for balance. Hold the horn loosely, with your thumb on top. Push on the horn as your horse gets into the ground for a hard stop, then pull on it as he gets out of a turn and pushes off in a new direction.

Cutting the Cow

The rules of cutting state that a contestant must execute a deep cut at least once during the two and one-half minutes involved. A deep cut implies that you ride your horse all the way to the back fence, drive several cows forward out of the herd, then choose one of those cows.

Most cutters cut deep as their run begins, thereby making sure that they have plenty of time to do the job correctly.

The most important thing about cutting a cow out of the herd is to remain relaxed but alert. Many beginner cutters get tense when they enter a herd of cattle. Their nervousness leads them to handle the horse roughly. Things get rushed and the cattle get tense. They move fast and become difficult to cut. Move your horse slowly. Stop every few strides if you need to, to look the cattle over. If you take your time, you will have plenty of time to show your horse to the judges.

Your goal when cutting a cow is to end up in the center of the arena, with your horse facing the cow and the cow either standing or moving slowly. If the cow is running hard, back and forth across the arena, you will likely have to pick up on your horse to "lock" him onto the cow. This may cost you points. However, if your horse is facing the cow when you begin your cut, it is easier for him to go either left or right. Consequently, he begins his work with a working advantage over the cow rather than the disadvantage of having to do a hard stop and turn.

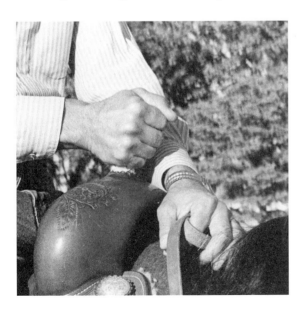

Hold your rein hand on the horse's neck, in front of the saddle pad. Hold the horn with your other hand. Your elbow should be next to your hip. Your arm should be relaxed and act only when necessary, pushing on the horn when your horse goes into a stop and pulling on the horn when he pushes hard out of a stop.

So ride deep to the back fence and drive about half the herd out thirty feet or so in front of the back fence. Again, take plenty or time and move as slowly as necessary to keep the cattle quiet.

Choose a cow from among those in front of you. Do not try to cut a charging cow. Even if you were successful in cutting off one of those trying to rush back immediately to the herd, she would be very difficult (if not impossible) to handle when she became the only cow remaining in front of your horse. Rather, let the eager ones run back to the herd. Select one of the cows that is aware of you and your horse between her and the herd, but is not panicking about it. These cattle are not as likely to try to run under your horse to get back to the herd.

Keep your horse's head even with the head of the cow you choose to cut. If at all possible, do this by sidepassing your horse left and right as the small bunch of cattle moves in front of you. Sidepassing your horse to control your cut offers two advantages: first, if you have body control of your horse, sidepassing is quieter than the turns and therefore does not disturb the cut as much. Second, and the main advantage of this method, sidepassing leaves your horse head-to-head with the cow when all the other cattle have peeled back to the herd. Put your rein hand down on his withers and let him do his job. Everything happens quietly. No running left or right. No penalties for reining your horse.

Keeping these basics of riding the cutting horse in mind, get on your horse, ride deep in the herd, and drive out a few cows. Take the one that stands there looking at you, then settle down in the best seat in the house.

Epilogue

If you have studied the entire book, congratulations! You probably were quite familiar with some topics, gained some insight into others, and are ready to work on them yourself. Go ahead and practice. Internalize the theory so that you can understand what happens, then ride, focusing on the feel.

There is no reason you cannot become as highly qualified a rider as you want to be. You too can become one of the most successful riders ever. Remember—none of us is born knowing how to ride a horse. All of us have had to learn how to do it.

The only barriers to your success at horsemanship are those that you yourself erect. Although time constraints or financial limitations may exist, you do not have to bow down to them. They are merely obstacles and—just like your trail horse—you can get around or over them. Your success at horsemanship comes from a day-by-day, step-by-step, thoughtful road map you draw for yourself. With your goal in mind, use the information in this book to better your and your horse's performance.

Glossary

Aids   The tools a rider uses to communicate his or her wishes to the horse. The natural aids are the seat, the hands, the legs, and the voice; the artificial aids are the spurs and the riding crop. Aids are either active or passive. Active aids are those that act on the horse for the purpose of executing a specific exercise or maneuver. Passive aids are those to which the horse does not need to respond.

Bending exercises   All exercises in which the horse is bent either left or right for the purpose of developing body control, suppleness, and strength.

Bitting devices   Also called *bitting instruments*. Tools designed to assist in the bitting of horses. Common bitting devices include draw reins, the German martingale, the running martingale, the standing martingale (tiedown), and the cavesson.

Body control   A definite goal in the schooling of the performance horse, body control is the desirable condition in which a rider can bend, balance, and otherwise position the horse's body, as necessary, with the complete and willing cooperation of the the horse.

Bosal   A teardrop-shaped device that fits around the horse's nose and jaw, just below the cheekbones. Bosals are usually made of braided rawhide.

Bridle path   The space behind the horse's ears in which the crown piece of the bridle runs over the mane.

Cheek pieces   The part of a snaffle bit to which the reins attach.

Curb strap/chain   Length of leather, rawhide, nylon, or chain that attaches to the bridle rings of the curb bit or to the cheek pieces of the snaffle bit.

Downward Transition   Any change from a faster to a slower gait, e.g., lope to trot.

Fall in   The action of the horse who tends to make a circle smaller than his rider wants. This horse is usually bent to the outside and pushes his shoulders against the inside rein.

Fall out   The action of the horse who tends to travel a circle larger than his rider wants. The horse who falls out of the circle pushes his shoulders against the outside rein and usually holds his body bent to the inside of the circle.

Green colts   Horses who have not yet attained a level of schooling where they flex laterally and longitudinally in response to the application of the rider's aids.

Guiding   The action of the horse as he responds to the light touch of the reins on each side of his neck and travels in the direction indicated by his rider. A horse is said to be guiding well when a subtle movement of the rein hand is sufficient to cause him to assume a new direction of travel.

Headstall   The part of the bridle that attaches to the bit on one side of the head, goes over the head, and attaches to the bit on the other side of the head.

Impulsion   The horse's natural desire to move with energy. Impulsion may also be generated by the rider. In either case, impulsion is essential to performance. The energetic movement of the horse can compensate for conformation weaknesses, but the well-conformed, lazy, and resentful horse cannot be positioned for optimum performance.

Independent seat   A rider whose hands, legs, and seat are totally independent from each other in their movement and who does not need to use his or her hands and stirrups to keep his or her center of gravity above that of the horse at all times is said to have an independent seat.

Lateral movements   Refers to suppling and body-control exercises, specifically: the pivot on the forehand, leg-yield, haunches-in, half-pass, shoulder-in, and sidepass.

Lunge line   A 20- to 30-foot length of cotton or nylon webbing, with a snap at one end and a handle at the other, used to exercise horses in a circle around the handler.

Midsection   The portion of the rider's body between the lowest ribs and the hip joint.

Mouthpiece   That part of any bit which runs across the horse's mouth.

Shanks   That part of a curb bit to which the reins, the headstall, and the curb strap attach.

Stimuli   Any agents or thoughts that arouse the mind. Incentives. Meaningless stimuli are any thoughts unrelated to the task at hand.

Upward Transition   Any change from a slower to a faster gait, e.g., walk to lope.

Index